Studies In Pessimism

By
Arthur Schopenhauer

The Essays Of Arthur Schopenhauer; Studies In Pessimism
ON THE SUFFERINGS OF THE WORLD.

Unless suffering is the direct and immediate object of life, our existence must entirely fail of its aim. It is absurd to look upon the enormous amount of pain that abounds everywhere in the world, and originates in needs and necessities inseparable from life itself, as serving no purpose at all and the result of mere chance. Each separate misfortune, as it comes, seems, no doubt, to be something exceptional; but misfortune in general is the rule.

I know of no greater absurdity than that propounded by most systems of philosophy in declaring evil to be negative in its character. Evil is just what is positive; it makes its own existence felt. Leibnitz is particularly concerned to defend this absurdity; and he seeks to strengthen his position by using a palpable and paltry sophism. It is the good which is negative; in other words, happiness and satisfaction always imply some desire fulfilled, some state of pain brought to an end.

This explains the fact that we generally find pleasure to be not nearly so pleasant as we expected, and pain very much more painful.

The pleasure in this world, it has been said, outweighs the pain; or, at any rate, there is an even balance between the two. If the reader wishes to see shortly whether this statement is true, let him compare the respective feelings of two animals, one of which is engaged in eating the other.

The best consolation in misfortune or affliction of any kind will be the thought of other people who are in a still worse plight than yourself; and this is a form of consolation open to every one. But what an awful fate this means for mankind as a whole!

We are like lambs in a field, disporting themselves under the eye of the butcher, who chooses out first one and then another for his prey. So it is that in our good days we are all unconscious of the evil Fate may have presently in store for us—sickness, poverty, mutilation, loss of sight or reason.

No little part of the torment of existence lies in this, that Time is continually pressing upon us, never letting us take breath, but always coming after us, like a taskmaster with a whip. If at any moment Time stays his hand, it is only when we are delivered over to the misery of boredom.

But misfortune has its uses; for, as our bodily frame would burst asunder if the pressure of the atmosphere was removed, so, if the lives of men were relieved of all need, hardship and adversity; if everything they took in hand were successful, they would be so swollen with arrogance that, though they might not burst, they would present the spectacle of unbridled folly—nay, they would go mad. And I may say, further, that a certain amount of care or pain or trouble is necessary for every man at all times. A ship without ballast is unstable and will not go straight.

Certain it is that work, worry, labor and trouble, form the lot of almost all men their whole life long. But if all wishes were fulfilled as soon as they arose, how would men occupy their lives? what would they do with their time? If the world were a paradise of luxury and ease, a land flowing with milk and honey, where every Jack obtained his Jill at once and without any difficulty, men would either die of boredom or hang themselves; or there would be wars, massacres, and murders; so that in the end mankind would inflict more suffering on itself than it has now to accept at the hands of Nature.

In early youth, as we contemplate our coming life, we are like children in a theatre before the curtain is raised, sitting there in high spirits and eagerly waiting for the play to begin. It is a blessing that we do not know what is really going to happen. Could we foresee it, there are times when children might seem like innocent prisoners, condemned, not to death, but to life, and as yet all unconscious of what their sentence means. Nevertheless, every man desires to reach old age; in other words, a state of life of which it may be said: "It is bad to-day, and it will be worse to-morrow; and so on till the worst of all."

If you try to imagine, as nearly as you can, what an amount of misery, pain and suffering of every kind the sun shines upon in its course, you will admit that it would be much better if, on the earth as little as on the moon, the sun were able to call forth the phenomena of life; and if, here as there, the surface were still in a crystalline state.

Again, you may look upon life as an unprofitable episode, disturbing the blessed calm of non-existence. And, in any case, even though things have gone with you tolerably well, the longer you live the more clearly you will feel that, on the whole, life is a disappointment, nay, a cheat.

If two men who were friends in their youth meet again when they are old, after being separated for a life-time, the chief feeling they will have at the sight of each other will be one of complete disappointment at life as a whole; because their thoughts will be carried back to that earlier time when life seemed so fair as it lay spread out before them in the rosy light of dawn, promised so much—and then performed so little. This feeling will so completely predominate over every other that they will not even consider it necessary to give it words; but on either side it will be silently assumed, and form the ground-work of all they have to talk about.

He who lives to see two or three generations is like a man who sits some time in the conjurer's booth at a fair, and witnesses the performance twice or thrice in succession. The tricks were meant to be seen only once; and when they are no longer a novelty and cease to deceive, their effect is gone.

While no man is much to be envied for his lot, there are countless numbers whose fate is to be deplored.

Life is a task to be done. It is a fine thing to say defunctus est; it means that the man has done his task.

If children were brought into the world by an act of pure reason alone, would the human race continue to exist? Would not a man rather have so much sympathy with the coming generation as to spare it the burden of existence? or at any rate not take it upon himself to impose that burden upon it in cold blood.

I shall be told, I suppose, that my philosophy is comfortless—because I speak the truth; and people prefer to be assured that everything the Lord has made is good. Go to the priests, then, and leave philosophers in peace! At any rate, do not ask us to accommodate our doctrines to the lessons you have been taught. That is what those rascals of sham philosophers will do for you. Ask them for any doctrine you please, and you will get it. Your University professors are bound to preach optimism; and it is an easy and agreeable task to upset their theories.

I have reminded the reader that every state of welfare, every feeling of satisfaction, is negative in its character; that is to say, it consists in freedom from pain, which is the positive element of existence. It follows, therefore, that the happiness of any given life is to be measured, not by its joys and pleasures, but by the extent to which it has been free from suffering—from positive evil. If this is the true standpoint, the lower animals appear to enjoy a happier destiny than man. Let us examine the matter a little more closely.

However varied the forms that human happiness and misery may take, leading a man to seek the one and shun the other, the material basis of it all is bodily pleasure or bodily pain. This basis is very restricted: it is simply health, food, protection from wet and cold, the satisfaction of the sexual instinct; or else the absence of these things. Consequently, as far as real physical pleasure is concerned, the man is not better off than the brute, except in so far as the higher possibilities of his nervous system make him more sensitive to every kind of pleasure, but also, it must be remembered, to every kind of pain. But then compared with the brute, how much stronger are the passions aroused in him! what an immeasurable difference there is in the depth and vehemence of his emotions!—and yet, in the one case, as in the other, all to produce the same result in the end: namely, health, food, clothing, and so on.

The chief source of all this passion is that thought for what is absent and future, which, with man, exercises such a powerful influence upon all he does. It is this that is the real origin of his cares, his hopes, his fears— emotions which affect him much more deeply than could ever be the case with those present joys and sufferings to which the brute is confined. In his powers of reflection, memory and foresight, man possesses, as it were, a machine for condensing and storing up his pleasures and his sorrows. But the brute has nothing of the kind; whenever it is in pain, it is as though it were suffering for the first time, even though the same thing should have previously happened to it times out of number. It has no power of summing up its feelings. Hence its careless and placid temper: how much it is to be envied! But in man reflection comes in, with all the emotions to which it gives rise; and taking up the same elements of pleasure and pain which are common to him and the brute, it develops his susceptibility to happiness and misery to such a degree that, at one moment the man is brought in an instant to a state of delight that may even prove fatal, at another to the depths of despair and suicide.

If we carry our analysis a step farther, we shall find that, in order to increase his pleasures, man has intentionally added to the number and pressure of his needs, which in their original state were not much more difficult to satisfy than those of the brute. Hence luxury in all its forms; delicate food, the use of tobacco and opium, spirituous liquors, fine clothes, and the thousand and one things than he considers necessary to his existence.

And above and beyond all this, there is a separate and peculiar source of pleasure, and consequently of pain, which man has established for himself, also as the result of using his powers of reflection; and this occupies him out of all proportion to its value, nay, almost more than all his other interests put together—I mean ambition and the feeling of honor and shame; in plain words, what he thinks about the opinion other people have of him. Taking a thousand forms, often very strange ones, this becomes the goal of almost all the efforts he makes that are not rooted in physical pleasure or pain. It is true that besides the sources of pleasure which he has in common with the brute, man has the pleasures of the mind as well. These admit of many gradations, from the most innocent trifling or the merest talk up to the highest intellectual achievements; but there is the accompanying boredom to be set against them on the side of suffering. Boredom is a form of suffering unknown to brutes, at any rate in their natural state; it is only the very cleverest of them who show faint traces of it when they are domesticated; whereas in the case of man it has become a downright scourge. The crowd of miserable wretches whose one aim in life is to fill their purses but never to put anything into their heads, offers a singular instance of this torment of boredom. Their wealth becomes a punishment by delivering them up to misery of having nothing to do; for, to escape it, they will rush about in all directions, traveling here, there and everywhere. No sooner do they arrive in a place than they are anxious to know what amusements it affords; just as though they were beggars asking where they could receive a dole! Of a truth, need and boredom are the two poles of human life. Finally, I may mention that as regards the sexual relation, a man is committed to a peculiar arrangement which drives him obstinately to choose one person. This feeling grows, now and then, into a more or less passionate love, which is the source of little pleasure and much suffering.

It is, however, a wonderful thing that the mere addition of thought should serve to raise such a vast and lofty structure of human happiness and misery; resting, too, on the same narrow basis of joy and sorrow as man holds in common with the brute, and exposing him to such violent emotions, to so many storms of passion, so much convulsion of feeling, that what he has suffered stands written and may be read in the lines on his face. And yet, when all is told, he has been struggling ultimately for the very same things as the brute has attained, and with an incomparably smaller expenditure of passion and pain.

But all this contributes to increase the measures of suffering in human life out of all proportion to its pleasures; and the pains of life are made much worse for man by the fact that death is something very real to him. The brute flies from death instinctively without really knowing what it is, and therefore without ever contemplating it in the way natural to a man, who has this prospect always before his eyes. So that even if only a few brutes die a natural death, and most of them live only just long enough to transmit their species, and then, if not earlier, become the prey of some other animal,—whilst man, on the other hand, manages to make so-called natural death the rule, to which, however, there are a good many exceptions,—the advantage is on the side of the brute, for the reason stated above. But the fact is that man attains the natural term of years just as seldom as the brute; because the unnatural way in which he lives, and the strain of work and emotion, lead to a degeneration of the race; and so his goal is not often reached.

The brute is much more content with mere existence than man; the plant is wholly so; and man finds satisfaction in it just in proportion as he is dull and obtuse. Accordingly, the life of the brute carries less of sorrow with it, but also less of joy, when compared with the life of man; and while this may be traced, on the one side, to freedom from the torment of care andanxiety, it is also due to the fact that hope, in any real sense, is unknown to the brute. It is thus deprived of any share in that which gives us the most and best of our joys and pleasures, the mental anticipation of a happy future, and the inspiriting play of phantasy, both of which we owe to our power of imagination. If the brute is free from care, it is also, in this sense, without hope; in either case, because its consciousness is limited to the present moment, to what it can actually see before it. The brute is an embodiment of present impulses, and hence what elements of fear and hope exist in its nature—and they do not go very far—arise only in relation to objects that lie before it and within reach of those impulses: whereas a man's range of vision embraces the whole of his life, and extends far into the past and future.

Following upon this, there is one respect in which brutes show real wisdom when compared with us—I mean, their quiet, placid enjoyment of the present moment. The tranquillity of mind which this seems to give them often puts us to shame for the many times we allow our thoughts and our cares to make us restless and discontented. And, in fact, those pleasures of hope and anticipation which I have been mentioning are not to be had for nothing. The delight which a man has in hoping for and looking forward to some special satisfaction is a part of the real pleasure attaching to it enjoyed in advance. This is afterwards deducted; for the more we look forward to anything, the less satisfaction we find in it when it comes. But the brute's enjoyment is not anticipated, and therefore, suffers no deduction; so that the actual pleasure of the moment comes to it whole and unimpaired. In the same way, too, evil presses upon the brute only with its own intrinsic weight; whereas with us the fear of its coming often makes its burden ten times more grievous.

It is just this characteristic way in which the brute gives itself up entirely to the present moment that contributes so much to the delight we take in our domestic pets. They are the present moment personified, and in some respects they make us feel the value of every hour that is free from trouble and annoyance, which we, with our thoughts and preoccupations, mostly disregard. But man, that selfish and heartless creature, misuses this quality of the brute to be more content than we are with mere existence, and often works it to such an extent that he allows the brute absolutely nothing more than mere, bare life. The bird which was made so that it might rove over half of the world, he shuts up into the space of a cubic foot, there to die a slow death in longing and crying for freedom; for in a cage it does not sing for the pleasure of it. And when I see how man misuses the dog, his best friend; how he ties up this intelligent animal with a chain, I feel the deepest sympathy with the brute and burning indignation against its master.

We shall see later that by taking a very high standpoint it is possible to justify the sufferings of mankind. But this justification cannot apply to animals, whose sufferings, while in a great measure brought about by men, are often considerable even apart from their agency. And so we are forced to ask, Why and for what purpose does all this torment and agony exist? There is nothing here to give the will pause; it is not free to deny itself and so obtain redemption. There is only one consideration that may serve to explain the sufferings of animals. It is this: that the will to live, which underlies the whole world of phenomena, must, in their case satisfy its cravings by feeding upon itself. This it does by forming a gradation of phenomena, every one of which exists at the expense of another. I have shown, however, that the capacity for suffering is less in animals than in man. Any further explanation that may be given of their fate will be in the nature of hypothesis, if not actually mythical in its character; and I may leave the reader to speculate upon the matter for himself.

Brahma is said to have produced the world by a kind of fall or mistake; and in order to atone for his folly, he is bound to remain in it himself until he works out his redemption. As an account of the origin of things, that is admirable! According to the doctrines of Buddhism, the world came into being as the result of some inexplicable disturbance in the heavenly calm of Nirvana, that blessed state obtained by expiation, which had endured so long a time—the change taking place by a kind of fatality. This explanation must be understood as having at bottom some moral bearing; although it is illustrated by an exactly parallel theory in the domain of physical science, which places the origin of the sun in a primitive streak of mist, formed one knows not how. Subsequently, by a series of moral errors, the world became gradually worse and worse—true of the physical orders as well—until it assumed the dismal aspect it wears to-day. Excellent! The Greeks looked upon the world and the gods as the work of an inscrutable necessity. A passable explanation: we may be content with it until we can get a better. Again, Ormuzd and Ahriman are rival powers, continually at war. That is not bad. But that a God like Jehovah should have created this world of misery and woe, out of pure caprice, and because he enjoyed doing it, and should then have clapped his hands in praise of his own work, and declared everything to be very good—that will not do at all! In its explanation of the origin of the world, Judaism is inferior to any other form of religious doctrine professed by a civilized nation; and it is quite in keeping with this that it is the only one which presents no trace whatever of any belief in the immortality of the soul.

Even though Leibnitz' contention, that this is the best of all possible worlds, were correct, that would not justify God in having created it. For he is the Creator not of the world only, but of possibility itself; and, therefore, he ought to have so ordered possibility as that it would admit of something better.

There are two things which make it impossible to believe that this world is the successful work of an all-wise, all-good, and, at the same time, all-powerful Being; firstly, the misery which abounds in it everywhere; and secondly, the obvious imperfection of its highest product, man, who is a burlesque of what he should be. These things cannot be reconciled with any such belief. On the contrary, they are just the facts which support what

I have been saying; they are our authority for viewing the world as the outcome of our own misdeeds, and therefore, as something that had better not have been. Whilst, under the former hypothesis, they amount to a bitter accusation against the Creator, and supply material for sarcasm; under the latter they form an indictment against our own nature, our own will, and teach us a lesson of humility. They lead us to see that, like the children of a libertine, we come into the world with the burden of sin upon us; and that it is only through having continually to atone for this sin that our existence is so miserable, and that its end is death.

There is nothing more certain than the general truth that it is the grievous sin of the world which has produced the grievous suffering of the world. I am not referring here to the physical connection between these two things lying in the realm of experience; my meaning is metaphysical. Accordingly, the sole thing that reconciles me to the Old Testament is the story of the Fall. In my eyes, it is the only metaphysical truth in that book, even though it appears in the form of an allegory. There seems to me no better explanation of our existence than that it is the result of some false step, some sin of which we are paying the penalty. I cannot refrain from recommending the thoughtful reader a popular, but at the same time, profound treatise on this subject by Claudius which exhibits the essentially pessimistic spirit of Christianity. It is entitled: Cursed is the ground for thy sake.

Between the ethics of the Greeks and the ethics of the Hindoos, there is a glaring contrast. In the one case (with the exception, it must be confessed, of Plato), the object of ethics is to enable a man to lead a happy life; in the other, it is to free and redeem him from life altogether—as is directly stated in the very first words of the Sankhya Karika.

Allied with this is the contrast between the Greek and the Christian idea of death. It is strikingly presented in a visible form on a fine antique sarcophagus in the gallery of Florence, which exhibits, in relief, the whole series of ceremonies attending a wedding in ancient times, from the formal offer to the evening when Hymen's torch lights the happy couple home. Compare with that the Christian coffin, draped in mournful black and surmounted with a crucifix! How much significance there is in these two ways of finding comfort in death. They are opposed to each other, but each is right. The one points to the affirmation of the will to live, which remains sure of life for all time, however rapidly its forms may change. The other, in the symbol of suffering and death, points to the denial of the will to live, to redemption from this world, the domain of death and devil. And in the question between the affirmation and the denial of the will to live, Christianity is in the last resort right.

The contrast which the New Testament presents when compared with the Old, according to the ecclesiastical view of the matter, is just that existing between my ethical system and the moral philosophy of Europe. The Old Testament represents man as under the dominion of Law, in which, however, there is no redemption. The New Testament declares Law to have failed, frees man from its dominion, and in its stead preaches the kingdom of grace, to be won by faith, love of neighbor and entire sacrifice of self. This is the path of redemption from the evil of the world. The spirit of the New Testament is undoubtedly asceticism, however your protestants and rationalists may twist it to suit their purpose. Asceticism is the denial of the will to live; and the transition from the Old Testament to the New, from the dominion of Law to that of Faith, from justification by works to redemption through the Mediator, from the domain of sin and death to eternal life in Christ, means, when taken in its real sense, the transition from the merely moral virtues to the denial of the will to live. My philosophy shows the metaphysical foundation of justice and the love of mankind, and points to the goal to which these virtues necessarily lead, if they are practised in perfection. At the same time it is candid in confessing that a man must turn his back upon the world, and that the denial of the will to live is the way of redemption. It is therefore really at one with the spirit of the New Testament, whilst all other systems are couched in the spirit of the Old; that is to say, theoretically as well as practically, their result is Judaism — mere despotic theism. In this sense, then, my doctrine might be called the only true Christian philosophy — however paradoxical a statement this may seem to people who take superficial views instead of penetrating to the heart of the matter.

If you want a safe compass to guide you through life, and to banish all doubt as to the right way of looking at it, you cannot do better than accustom yourself to regard this world as a penitentiary, a sort of a penal colony, or [Greek: ergastaerion] as the earliest philosopher called it. Amongst the Christian Fathers, Origen, with praiseworthy courage, took this view,[2] which is further justified by certain objective theories of life. I refer, not to my own philosophy alone, but to the wisdom of all ages, as expressed in Brahmanism and Buddhism, and in the sayings of Greek philosophers like Empedocles and Pythagoras; as also by Cicero, in his remark that the wise men of old used to teach that we come into this world to pay the penalty of crime committed in another state of existence—a doctrine which formed part of the initiation into the mysteries.[3] And Vanini—whom his contemporaries burned, finding that an easier task than to confute him—puts the same thing in a very forcible way. Man, he says, is so full of every kind of misery that, were it not repugnant to the Christian religion, I should venture to affirm that if evil spirits exist at all, they have posed into human form and are now atoning for their crimes.[4] And true Christianity—using the word in its right sense—also regards our existence as the consequence of sin and error.

If you accustom yourself to this view of life you will regulate your expectations accordingly, and cease to look upon all its disagreeable incidents, great and small, its sufferings, its worries, its misery, as anything unusual or irregular; nay, you will find that everything is as it should be, in a world where each of us pays the penalty of existence in his own peculiar way. Amongst the evils of a penal colony is the society of those who form it; and if the reader is worthy of better company, he will need no words from me to remind him of what he has to put up with at present. If he has a soul above the common, or if he is a man of genius, he will occasionally feel like some noble prisoner of state, condemned to work in the galleys with common criminals; and he will follow his example and try to isolate himself.

In general, however, it should be said that this view of life will enable us to contemplate the so-called imperfections of the great majority of men, their moral and intellectual deficiencies and the resulting base type of countenance, without any surprise, to say nothing of indignation; for we shall never cease to reflect where we are, and that the men about us are beings conceived and born in sin, and living to atone for it. That is what Christianity means in speaking of the sinful nature of man.

Pardon's the word to all! Whatever folly men commit, be their shortcomings or their vices what they may, let us exercise forbearance; remembering that when these faults appear in others, it is our follies and vices that we behold. They are the shortcomings of humanity, to which we belong; whose faults, one and all, we share; yes, even those very faults at which we now wax so indignant, merely because they have not yet appeared in ourselves. They are faults that do not lie on the surface. But they exist down there in the depths of our nature; and should anything call them forth, they will come and show themselves, just as we now see them in others. One man, it is true, may have faults that are absent in his fellow; and it is undeniable that the sum total of bad qualities is in some cases very large; for the difference of individuality between man and man passes all measure.

In fact, the conviction that the world and man is something that had better not have been, is of a kind to fill us with indulgence towards one another. Nay, from this point of view, we might well consider the proper form of address to be, not Monsieur, Sir, mein Herr, but my fellow-sufferer, Socî malorum, compagnon de miseres! This may perhaps sound strange, but it is in keeping with the facts; it puts others in a right light; and it reminds us of that which is after all the most necessary thing in life—the tolerance, patience, regard, and love of neighbor, of which everyone stands in need, and which, therefore, every man owes to his fellow.

THE VANITY OF EXISTENCE.

This vanity finds expression in the whole way in which things exist; in the infinite nature of Time and Space, as opposed to the finite nature of the individual in both; in the ever-passing present moment as the only mode of actual existence; in the interdependence and relativity of all things; in continual Becoming without ever Being; in constant wishing and never being satisfied; in the long battle which forms the history of life, where every effort is checked by difficulties, and stopped until they are overcome. Time is that in which all things pass away; it is merely the form under which the will to live—the thing-in-itself and therefore imperishable—has revealed to it that its efforts are in vain; it is that agent by which at every moment all things in our hands become as nothing, and lose any real value they possess.

That which has been exists no more; it exists as little as that which has never been. But of everything that exists you must say, in the next moment, that it has been. Hence something of great importance now past is inferior to something of little importance now present, in that the latter is a reality, and related to the former as something to nothing.

A man finds himself, to his great astonishment, suddenly existing, after thousands and thousands of years of non-existence: he lives for a little while; and then, again, comes an equally long period when he must exist no more. The heart rebels against this, and feels that it cannot be true. The crudest intellect cannot speculate on such a subject without having a presentiment that Time is something ideal in its nature. This ideality of Time and Space is the key to every true system of metaphysics; because it provides for quite another order of things than is to be met with in the domain of nature. This is why Kant is so great.

Of every event in our life we can say only for one moment that it is; for ever after, that it was. Every evening we are poorer by a day. It might, perhaps, make us mad to see how rapidly our short span of time ebbs away; if it were not that in the furthest depths of our being we are secretly conscious of our share in the exhaustible spring of eternity, so that we can always hope to find life in it again.

Consideration of the kind, touched on above, might, indeed, lead us to embrace the belief that the greatest wisdom is to make the enjoyment of the present the supreme object of life; because that is the only reality, all else being merely the play of thought. On the other hand, such a course might just as well be called the greatest folly: for that which in the next moment exists no more, and vanishes utterly, like a dream, can never be worth a serious effort.

The whole foundation on which our existence rests is the present—the ever-fleeting present. It lies, then, in the very nature of our existence to take the form of constant motion, and to offer no possibility of our ever attaining the rest for which we are always striving. We are like a man running downhill, who cannot keep on his legs unless he runs on, and will inevitably fall if he stops; or, again, like a pole balanced on the tip of one's finger; or like a planet, which would fall into its sun the moment it ceased to hurry forward on its way. Unrest is the mark of existence.

In a world where all is unstable, and nought can endure, but is swept onwards at once in the hurrying whirlpool of change; where a man, if he is to keep erect at all, must always be advancing and moving, like an acrobat on a rope—in such a world, happiness in inconceivable. How can it dwell where, as Plato says, continual Becoming and never Being is the sole form of existence? In the first place, a man never is happy, but spends his whole life in striving after something which he thinks will make him so; he seldom attains his goal, and when he does, it is only to be disappointed; he is mostly shipwrecked in the end, and comes into harbor with masts and rigging gone. And then, it is all one whether he has been happy or miserable; for his life was never anything more than a present moment always vanishing; and now it is over.

At the same time it is a wonderful thing that, in the world of human beings as in that of animals in general, this manifold restless motion is produced and kept up by the agency of two simple impulses—hunger and the sexual instinct; aided a little, perhaps, by the influence of boredom, but by nothing else; and that, in the theatre of life, these suffice to form the primum mobile of how complicated a machinery, setting in motion how strange and varied a scene!

On looking a little closer, we find that inorganic matter presents a constant conflict between chemical forces, which eventually works dissolution; and on the other hand, that organic life is impossible without continual change of matter, and cannot exist if it does not receive perpetual help from without. This is the realm of finality; and its opposite would be an infinite existence, exposed to no attack from without, and needing nothing to support it; [Greek: haei hosautos dn], the realm of eternal peace; [Greek: oute giguomenon oute apollumenon], some timeless, changeless state, one and undiversified; the negative knowledge of which forms the dominant note of the Platonic philosophy. It is to some such state as this that the denial of the will to live opens up the way.

The scenes of our life are like pictures done in rough mosaic. Looked at close, they produce no effect. There is nothing beautiful to be found in them, unless you stand some distance off. So, to gain anything we have longed for is only to discover how vain and empty it is; and even though we are always living in expectation of better things, at the same time we often repent and long to have the past back again. We look upon the present as something to be put up with while it lasts, and serving only as the way towards our goal. Hence most people, if they glance back when they come to the end of life, will find that all along they have been living ad interim: they will be surprised to find that the very thing they disregarded and let slip by unenjoyed, was just the life in the expectation of which they passed all their time. Of how many a man may it not be said that hope made a fool of him until he danced into the arms of death!

Then again, how insatiable a creature is man! Every satisfaction he attains lays the seeds of some new desire, so that there is no end to the wishes of each individual will. And why is this? The real reason is simply that, taken in itself, Will is the lord of all worlds: everything belongs to it, and therefore no one single thing can ever give it satisfaction, but only the whole, which is endless. For all that, it must rouse our sympathy to think how very little the Will, this lord of the world, really gets when it takes the form of an individual; usually only just enough to keep the body together. This is why man is so very miserable.

Life presents itself chiefly as a task—the task, I mean, of subsisting at all, gagner sa vie. If this is accomplished, life is a burden, and then there comes the second task of doing something with that which has been won—of warding off boredom, which, like a bird of prey, hovers over us, ready to fall wherever it sees a life secure from need. The first task is to win something; the second, to banish the feeling that it has been won; otherwise it is a burden.

Human life must be some kind of mistake. The truth of this will be sufficiently obvious if we only remember that man is a compound of needs and necessities hard to satisfy; and that even when they are satisfied, all he obtains is a state of painlessness, where nothing remains to him but abandonment to boredom. This is direct proof that existence has no real value in itself; for what is boredom but the feeling of the emptiness of life? If life—the craving for which is the very essence of our being—were possessed of any positive intrinsic value, there would be no such thing as boredom at all: mere existence would satisfy us in itself, and we should want for nothing. But as it is, we take no delight in existence except when we are struggling for something; and then distance and difficulties to be overcome make our goal look as though it would satisfy us—an illusion which vanishes when we reach it; or else when we are occupied with some purely intellectual interest—when in reality we have stepped forth from life to look upon it from the outside, much after the manner of spectators at a play. And even sensual pleasure itself means nothing but a struggle and aspiration, ceasing the moment its aim is attained. Whenever we are not occupied in one of these ways, but cast upon existence itself, its vain and worthless nature is brought home to us; and this is what we mean by boredom. The hankering after what is strange and uncommon—an innate and ineradicable tendency of human nature—shows how glad we are at any interruption of that natural course of affairs which is so very tedious.

That this most perfect manifestation of the will to live, the human organism, with the cunning and complex working of its machinery, must fall to dust and yield up itself and all its strivings to extinction — this is the naïve way in which Nature, who is always so true and sincere in what she says, proclaims the whole struggle of this will as in its very essence barren and unprofitable. Were it of any value in itself, anything unconditioned and absolute, it could not thus end in mere nothing.

If we turn from contemplating the world as a whole, and, in particular, the generations of men as they live their little hour of mock-existence and then are swept away in rapid succession; if we turn from this, and look at life in its small details, as presented, say, in a comedy, how ridiculous it all seems! It is like a drop of water seen through a microscope, a single drop teeming with infusoria; or a speck of cheese full of mites invisible to the naked eye. How we laugh as they bustle about so eagerly, and struggle with one another in so tiny a space! And whether here, or in the little span of human life, this terrible activity produces a comic effect.

It is only in the microscope that our life looks so big. It is an indivisible point, drawn out and magnified by the powerful lenses of Time and Space.

ON SUICIDE.

As far as I know, none but the votaries of monotheistic, that is to say, Jewish religions, look upon suicide as a crime. This is all the more striking, inasmuch as neither in the Old nor in the New Testament is there to be found any prohibition or positive disapproval of it; so that religious teachers are forced to base their condemnation of suicide on philosophical grounds of their own invention. These are so very bad that writers of this kind endeavor to make up for the weakness of their arguments by the strong terms in which they express their abhorrence of the practice; in other words, they declaim against it. They tell us that suicide is the greatest piece of cowardice; that only a madman could be guilty of it; and other insipidities of the same kind; or else they make the nonsensical remark that suicide is wrong; when it is quite obvious that there is nothing in the world to which every mail has a more unassailable title than to his own life and person.

Suicide, as I have said, is actually accounted a crime; and a crime which, especially under the vulgar bigotry that prevails in England, is followed by an ignominious burial and the seizure of the man's property; and for that reason, in a case of suicide, the jury almost always brings in a verdict of insanity. Now let the reader's own moral feelings decide as to whether or not suicide is a criminal act. Think of the impression that would be made upon you by the news that some one you know had committed the crime, say, of murder or theft, or been guilty of some act of cruelty or deception; and compare it with your feelings when you hear that he has met a voluntary death. While in the one case a lively sense of indignation and extreme resentment will be aroused, and you will call loudly for punishment or revenge, in the other you will be moved to grief and sympathy; and mingled with your thoughts will be admiration for his courage, rather than the moral disapproval which follows upon a wicked action. Who has not had acquaintances, friends, relations, who of their own free will have left this world; and are these to be thought of with horror as criminals? Most emphatically, No! I am rather of opinion that the clergy should be challenged to explain what right they have to go into the pulpit, or take up their pens, and stamp as a crime an action which many men whom we hold in affection and honor have committed; and to refuse an honorable burial to those who relinquish this world voluntarily. They have no Biblical authority to boast of, as justifying their condemnation of suicide; nay, not even any philosophical arguments that will hold water; and it must be understood that it is arguments we want, and that we will not be put off with mere phrases or words of abuse. If the criminal law forbids suicide, that is not an argument valid in the Church; and besides, the prohibition is ridiculous; for what penalty can frighten a man who is not afraid of death itself? If the law punishes people for trying to commit suicide, it is punishing the want of skill that makes the attempt a failure.

The ancients, moreover, were very far from regarding the matter in that light. Pliny says: Life is not so desirable a thing as to be protracted at any cost. Whoever you are, you are sure to die, even though your life has been full of abomination and crime. The chief of all remedies for a troubled mind is the feeling that among the blessings which Nature gives to man, there is none greater than an opportune death; and the best of it is that every one can avail himself of it. And elsewhere the same writer declares: Not even to God are all things possible; for he could not compass his own death, if he willed to die, and yet in all the miseries of our earthly life, this is the best of his gifts to man.[2] Nay, in Massilia and on the isle of Ceos, the man who could give valid reasons for relinquishing his life, was handed the cup of hemlock by the magistrate; and that, too, in public.[3] And in ancient times, how many heroes and wise men died a voluntary death. Aristotle,[4] it is true, declared suicide to be an offence against the State, although not against the person; but in Stobaeus' exposition of the Peripatetic philosophy there is the following remark: The good man should flee life when his misfortunes become too great; the bad man, also, when he is too prosperous. And similarly: So he will marry and beget children and take part in the affairs of the State, and, generally, practice virtue and continue to live; and then, again, if need be, and at any time necessity compels him, he will depart to his place of refuge in the tomb.[5] And we find that the Stoics actually praised suicide as a noble and heroic action, as hundreds of passages show; above all in the works of Seneca, who expresses the strongest approval of it. As is well known, the Hindoos look upon suicide as a religious act, especially when it takes the form of self-immolation by widows; but also when it consists in casting oneself under the wheels of the chariot of the god at Juggernaut, or being eaten by crocodiles in the Ganges, or being drowned in the holy tanks in the temples, and so on. The same thing occurs on the stage—that mirror of life. For example, in L'Orphelin de la Chine[6] a celebrated Chinese play, almost all the noble characters end by suicide; without the slightest hint anywhere, or any impression being produced on the spectator, that they are committing a crime. And in our own theatre it is much the same—Palmira, for instance, in Mahomet, or Mortimer in Maria Stuart, Othello, Countess Terzky.[7] Is Hamlet's monologue the meditation of a criminal? He merely declares that if we had any certainty of being annihilated by it, death would be infinitely preferable to the world as it is. But there lies the rub!

The reasons advanced against suicide by the clergy of monotheistic, that is to say, Jewish religions, and by those philosophers who adapt themselves thereto, are weak sophisms which can easily be refuted. The most thorough-going refutation of them is given by Hume in his Essay on Suicide. This did not appeal until after his death, when it was immediately suppressed, owing to the scandalous bigotry and outrageous ecclesiastical tyranny that prevailed in England; and hence only a very few copies of it were sold under cover of secrecy and at a high price. This and another treatise by that great man have come to us from Basle, and we may be thankful for the reprint.[2] It is a great disgrace to the English nation that a purely philosophical treatise, which, proceeding from one of the first thinkers and writers in England, aimed at refuting the current arguments against suicide by the light of cold reason, should be forced to sneak about in that country, as though it were some rascally production, until at last it found refuge on the Continent. At the same time it shows what a good conscience the Church has in such matters.

In my chief work I have explained the only valid reason existing against suicide on the score of mortality. It is this: that suicide thwarts the attainment of the highest moral aim by the fact that, for a real release from this world of misery, it substitutes one that is merely apparent. But from a mistake to a crime is a far cry; and it is as a crime that the clergy of Christendom wish us to regard suicide.

The inmost kernel of Christianity is the truth that suffering—the Cross—is the real end and object of life. Hence Christianity condemns suicide as thwarting this end; whilst the ancient world, taking a lower point of view, held it in approval, nay, in honor. But if that is to be accounted a valid reason against suicide, it involves the recognition of asceticism; that is to say, it is valid only from a much higher ethical standpoint than has ever been adopted by moral philosophers in Europe. If we abandon that high standpoint, there is no tenable reason left, on the score of morality, for condemning suicide. The extraordinary energy and zeal with which the clergy of monotheistic religions attack suicide is not supported either by any passages in the Bible or by any considerations of weight; so that it looks as though they must have some secret reason for their contention. May it not be this—that the voluntary surrender of life is a bad compliment for him who said that all things were very good? If this is so, it offers another instance of the crass optimism of these religions,—denouncing suicide to escape being denounced by it.

It will generally be found that, as soon as the terrors of life reach the point at which they outweigh the terrors of death, a man will put an end to his life. But the terrors of death offer considerable resistance; they stand like a sentinel at the gate leading out of this world. Perhaps there is no man alive who would not have already put an end to his life, if this end had been of a purely negative character, a sudden stoppage of existence. There is something positive about it; it is the destruction of the body; and a man shrinks from that, because his body is the manifestation of the will to live.

However, the struggle with that sentinel is, as a rule, not so hard as it may seem from a long way off, mainly in consequence of the antagonism between the ills of the body and the ills of the mind. If we are in great bodily pain, or the pain lasts a long time, we become indifferent to other troubles; all we think about is to get well. In the same way great mental suffering makes us insensible to bodily pain; we despise it; nay, if it should outweigh the other, it distracts our thoughts, and we welcome it as a pause in mental suffering. It is this feeling that makes suicide easy; for the bodily pain that accompanies it loses all significance in the eyes of one who is tortured by an excess of mental suffering. This is especially evident in the case of those who are driven to suicide by some purely morbid and exaggerated ill-humor. No special effort to overcome their feelings is necessary, nor do such people require to be worked up in order to take the step; but as soon as the keeper into whose charge they are given leaves them for a couple of minutes, they quickly bring their life to an end.

When, in some dreadful and ghastly dream, we reach the moment of greatest horror, it awakes us; thereby banishing all the hideous shapes that were born of the night. And life is a dream: when the moment of greatest horror compels us to break it off, the same thing happens.

Suicide may also be regarded as an experiment—a question which man puts to Nature, trying to force her to an answer. The question is this: What change will death produce in a man's existence and in his insight into the nature of things? It is a clumsy experiment to make; for it involves the destruction of the very consciousness which puts the question and awaits the answer.

IMMORTALITY: A DIALOGUE.
THRASYMACHOS — PHILALETHES.

Thrasymachos. Tell me now, in one word, what shall I be after my death? And mind you be clear and precise.

Philalethes. All and nothing!

Thrasymachos. I thought so! I gave you a problem, and you solve it by a contradiction. That's a very stale trick.

Philalethes. Yes, but you raise transcendental questions, and you expect me to answer them in language that is only made for immanent knowledge. It's no wonder that a contradiction ensues.

Thrasymachos. What do you mean by transcendental questions and immanent knowledge? I've heard these expressions before, of course; they are not new to me. The Professor was fond of using them, but only as predicates of the Deity, and he never talked of anything else; which was all quite right and proper. He argued thus: if the Deity was in the world itself, he was immanent; if he was somewhere outside it, he was transcendent. Nothing could be clearer and more obvious! You knew where you were. But this Kantian rigmarole won't do any more: it's antiquated and no longer applicable to modern ideas. Why, we've had a whole row of eminent men in the metropolis of German learning —

Philalethes. (Aside.) German humbug, he means.

Thrasymachos. The mighty Schleiermacher, for instance, and that gigantic intellect, Hegel; and at this time of day we've abandoned that nonsense. I should rather say we're so far beyond it that we can't put up with it any more. What's the use of it then? What does it all mean?

Philalethes. Transcendental knowledge is knowledge which passes beyond the bounds of possible experience, and strives to determine the nature of things as they are in themselves. Immanent knowledge, on the other hand, is knowledge which confines itself entirely with those bounds; so that it cannot apply to anything but actual phenomena. As far as you are an individual, death will be the end of you. But your individuality is not your true and inmost being: it is only the outward manifestation of it. It is not the thing-in-itself, but only the phenomenon presented in the form of time; and therefore with a beginning and an end. But your real being knows neither time, nor beginning, nor end, nor yet the limits of any given individual. It is everywhere present in every individual; and no individual can exist apart from it. So when death comes, on the one hand you are annihilated as an individual; on the other, you are and remain everything. That is what I meant when I said that after your death you would be all and nothing. It is difficult to find a more precise answer to your question and at the same time be brief. The answer is contradictory, I admit; but it is so simply because your life is in time, and the immortal part of you in eternity. You may put the matter thus: Your immortal part is something that does not last in time and yet is indestructible; but there you have another contradiction! You see what happens by trying to bring the transcendental within the limits of immanent knowledge. It is in some sort doing violence to the latter by misusing it for ends it was never meant to serve.

Thrasymachos. Look here, I shan't give twopence for your immortality unless I'm to remain an individual.

Philalethes. Well, perhaps I may be able to satisfy you on this point. Suppose I guarantee that after death you shall remain an individual, but only on condition that you first spend three months of complete unconsciousness.

Thrasymachos. I shall have no objection to that.

Philalethes. But remember, if people are completely unconscious, they take no account of time. So, when you are dead, it's all the same to you whether three months pass in the world of consciousness, or ten thousand years. In the one case as in the other, it is simply a matter of believing what is told you when you awake. So far, then, you can afford to be indifferent whether it is three months or ten thousand years that pass before you recover your individuality.

Thrasymachos. Yes, if it comes to that, I suppose you're right.

Philalethes. And if by chance, after those ten thousand years have gone by, no one ever thinks of awakening you, I fancy it would be no great misfortune. You would have become quite accustomed to non-existence after so long a spell of it—following upon such a very few years of life. At any rate you may be sure you would be perfectly ignorant of the whole thing. Further, if you knew that the mysterious power which keeps you in your present state of life had never once ceased in those ten thousand years to bring forth other phenomena like yourself, and to endow them with life, it would fully console you.

Thrasymachos. Indeed! So you think you're quietly going to do me out of my individuality with all this fine talk. But I'm up to your tricks. I tell you I won't exist unless I can have my individuality. I'm not going to be put off with 'mysterious powers,' and what you call 'phenomena.' I can't do without my individuality, and I won't give it up.

Philalethes. You mean, I suppose, that your individuality is such a delightful thing, so splendid, so perfect, and beyond compare—that you can't imagine anything better. Aren't you ready to exchange your present state for one which, if we can judge by what is told us, may possibly be superior and more endurable?

Thrasymachos. Don't you see that my individuality, be it what it may, is my very self? To me it is the most important thing in the world.

For God is God and I am I.

I want to exist, I, I. That's the main thing. I don't care about an existence which has to be proved to be mine, before I can believe it.

Philalethes. Think what you're doing! When you say I, I, I want to exist, it is not you alone that says this. Everything says it, absolutely everything that has the faintest trace of consciousness. It follows, then, that this desire of yours is just the part of you that is not individual—the part that is common to all things without distinction. It is the cry, not of the individual, but of existence itself; it is the intrinsic element in everything that exists, nay, it is the cause of anything existing at all. This desire craves for, and so is satisfied with, nothing less than existence in general—not any definite individual existence. No! that is not its aim. It seems to be so only because this desire—this Will—attains consciousness only in the individual, and therefore looks as though it were concerned with nothing but the individual. There lies the illusion—an illusion, it is true, in which the individual is held fast: but, if he reflects, he can break the fetters and set himself free. It is only indirectly, I say, that the individual has this violent craving for existence. It is the Will to Live which is the real and direct aspirant—alike and identical in all things. Since, then, existence is the free work, nay, the mere reflection of the will, where existence is, there, too, must be will; and for the moment the will finds its satisfaction in existence itself; so far, I mean, as that which never rests, but presses forward eternally, can ever find any satisfaction at all. The will is careless of the individual: the individual is not its business; although, as I have said, this seems to be the case, because the individual has no direct consciousness of will except in himself. The effect of this is to make the individual careful to maintain his own existence; and if this were not so, there would be no surety for the preservation of the species. From all this it is clear that individuality is not a form of perfection, but rather of limitation; and so to be freed from it is not loss but gain. Trouble yourself no more about the matter. Once thoroughly recognize what you are, what your existence really is, namely, the universal will to live, and the whole question will seem to you childish, and most ridiculous!

Thrasymachos. You're childish yourself and most ridiculous, like all philosophers! and if a man of my age lets himself in for a quarter-of-an-hour's talk with such fools, it is only because it amuses me and passes the time. I've more important business to attend to, so Good-bye.

PSYCHOLOGICAL OBSERVATIONS.

There is an unconscious propriety in the way in which, in all European languages, the word person is commonly used to denote a human being. The real meaning of persona is a mask, such as actors were accustomed to wear on the ancient stage; and it is quite true that no one shows himself as he is, but wears his mask and plays his part. Indeed, the whole of our social arrangements may be likened to a perpetual comedy; and this is why a man who is worth anything finds society so insipid, while a blockhead is quite at home in it.

Reason deserves to be called a prophet; for in showing us the consequence and effect of our actions in the present, does it not tell us what the future will be? This is precisely why reason is such an excellent power of restraint in moments when we are possessed by some base passion, some fit of anger, some covetous desire, that will lead us to do things whereof we must presently repent.

Hatred comes from the heart; contempt from the head; and neither feeling is quite within our control. For we cannot alter our heart; its basis is determined by motives; and our head deals with objective facts, and applies to them rules which are immutable. Any given individual is the union of a particular heart with a particular head.

Hatred and contempt are diametrically opposed and mutually exclusive. There are even not a few cases where hatred of a person is rooted in nothing but forced esteem for his qualities. And besides, if a man sets out to hate all the miserable creatures he meets, he will not have much energy left for anything else; whereas he can despise them, one and all, with the greatest ease. True, genuine contempt is just the reverse of true, genuine pride; it keeps quite quiet and gives no sign of its existence. For if a man shows that he despises you, he signifies at least this much regard for you, that he wants to let you know how little he appreciates you; and his wish is dictated by hatred, which cannot exist with real contempt. On the contrary, if it is genuine, it is simply the conviction that the object of it is a man of no value at all. Contempt is not incompatible with indulgent and kindly treatment, and for the sake of one's own peace and safety, this should not be omitted; it will prevent irritation; and there is no one who cannot do harm if he is roused to it. But if this pure, cold, sincere contempt ever shows itself, it will be met with the most truculent hatred; for the despised person is not in a position to fight contempt with its own weapons.

Melancholy is a very different thing from bad humor, and of the two, it is not nearly so far removed from a gay and happy temperament. Melancholy attracts, while bad humor repels.

Hypochondria is a species of torment which not only makes us unreasonably cross with the things of the present; not only fills us with groundless anxiety on the score of future misfortunes entirely of our own manufacture; but also leads to unmerited self-reproach for what we have done in the past.

Hypochondria shows itself in a perpetual hunting after things that vex and annoy, and then brooding over them. The cause of it is an inward morbid discontent, often co-existing with a naturally restless temperament. In their extreme form, this discontent and this unrest lead to suicide.

Any incident, however trivial, that rouses disagreeable emotion, leaves an after-effect in our mind, which for the time it lasts, prevents our taking a clear objective view of the things about us, and tinges all our thoughts: just as a small object held close to the eye limits and distorts our field of vision.

What makes people hard-hearted is this, that each man has, or fancies he has, as much as he can bear in his own troubles. Hence, if a man suddenly finds himself in an unusually happy position, it will in most cases result in his being sympathetic and kind. But if he has never been in any other than a happy position, or this becomes his permanent state, the effect of it is often just the contrary: it so far removes him from suffering that he is incapable of feeling any more sympathy with it. So it is that the poor often show themselves more ready to help than the rich.

At times it seems as though we both wanted and did not want the same thing, and felt at once glad and sorry about it. For instance, if on some fixed date we are going to be put to a decisive test about anything in which it would be a great advantage to us to come off victorious, we shall be anxious for it to take place at once, and at the same time we shall tremble at the thought of its approach. And if, in the meantime, we hear that, for once in a way, the date has been postponed, we shall experience a feeling both of pleasure and of annoyance; for the news is disappointing, but nevertheless it affords us momentary relief. It is just the same thing if we are expecting some important letter carrying a definite decision, and it fails to arrive.

In such cases there are really two different motives at work in us; the stronger but more distant of the two being the desire to stand the test and to have the decision given in our favor; and the weaker, which touches us more nearly, the wish to be left for the present in peace and quiet, and accordingly in further enjoyment of the advantage which at any rate attaches to a state of hopeful uncertainty, compared with the possibility that the issue may be unfavorable.

In my head there is a permanent opposition-party; and whenever I take any step or come to any decision—though I may have given the matter mature consideration—it afterwards attacks what I have done, without, however, being each time necessarily in the right. This is, I suppose, only a form of rectification on the part of the spirit of scrutiny; but it often reproaches me when I do not deserve it. The same thing, no doubt, happens to many others as well; for where is the man who can help thinking that, after all, it were better not to have done something that he did with great deliberation:

Quid tam dextro pede concipis ut te Conatus non poeniteat votique peracti?

Why is it that common is an expression of contempt? and that uncommon, extraordinary, distinguished, denote approbation? Why is everything that is common contemptible?

Common in its original meaning denotes that which is peculiar to all men, i.e., shared equally by the whole species, and therefore an inherent part of its nature. Accordingly, if an individual possesses no qualities beyond those which attach to mankind in general, he is a common man. Ordinary is a much milder word, and refers rather to intellectual character; whereas common has more of a moral application.

What value can a creature have that is not a whit different from millions of its kind? Millions, do I say? nay, an infiniture of creatures which, century after century, in never-ending flow, Nature sends bubbling up from her inexhaustible springs; as generous with them as the smith with the useless sparks that fly around his anvil.

It is obviously quite right that a creature which has no qualities except those of the species, should have to confine its claim to an existence entirely within the limits of the species, and live a life conditioned by those limits.

In various passages of my works, I have argued that whilst a lower animal possesses nothing more than the generic character of its species, man is the only being which can lay claim to possess an individual character. But in most men this individual character comes to very little in reality; and they may be almost all ranged under certain classes: ce sont des espèces. Their thoughts and desires, like their faces, are those of the species, or, at any rate, those of the class to which they belong; and accordingly, they are of a trivial, every-day, common character, and exist by the thousand. You can usually tell beforehand what they are likely to do and say. They have no special stamp or mark to distinguish them; they are like manufactured goods, all of a piece.

If, then, their nature is merged in that of the species, how shall their existence go beyond it? The curse of vulgarity puts men on a par with the lower animals, by allowing them none but a generic nature, a generic form of existence. Anything that is high or great or noble, must then, as a mater of course, and by its very nature, stand alone in a world where no better expression can be found to denote what is base and contemptible than that which I have mentioned as in general use, namely, common.

Will, as the thing-in-itself, is the foundation of all being; it is part and parcel of every creature, and the permanent element in everything. Will, then, is that which we possess in common with all men, nay, with all animals, and even with lower forms of existence; and in so far we are akin to everything—so far, that is, as everything is filled to overflowing with will. On the other hand, that which places one being over another, and sets differences between man and man, is intellect and knowledge; therefore in every manifestation of self we should, as far as possible, give play to the intellect alone; for, as we have seen, the will is the common part of us. Every violent exhibition of will is common and vulgar; in other words, it reduces us to the level of the species, and makes us a mere type and example of it; in that it is just the character of the species that we are showing. So every fit of anger is something common—every unrestrained display of joy, or of hate, or fear—in short, every form of emotion; in other words, every movement of the will, if it's so strong as decidedly to outweigh the intellectual element in consciousness, and to make the man appear as a being that wills rather than knows.

In giving way to emotion of this violent kind, the greatest genius puts himself on a level with the commonest son of earth. Contrarily, if a man desires to be absolutely uncommon, in other words, great, he should never allow his consciousness to be taken possession of and dominated by the movement of his will, however much he may be solicited thereto. For example, he must be able to observe that other people are badly disposed towards him, without feeling any hatred towards them himself; nay, there is no surer sign of a great mind than that it refuses to notice annoying and insulting expressions, but straightway ascribes them, as it ascribes countless other mistakes, to the defective knowledge of the speaker, and so merely observes without feeling them. This is the meaning of that remark of Gracian, that nothing is more unworthy of a man than to let it be seen that he is one—el mayor desdoro de un hombre es dar muestras de que es hombre.

And even in the drama, which is the peculiar province of the passions and emotions, it is easy for them to appear common and vulgar. And this is specially observable in the works of the French tragic writers, who set no other aim before themselves but the delineation of the passions; and by indulging at one moment in a vaporous kind of pathos which makes them ridiculous, at another in epigrammatic witticisms, endeavor to conceal the vulgarity of their subject. I remember seeing the celebrated Mademoiselle Rachel as Maria Stuart: and when she burst out in fury against Elizabeth—though she did it very well—I could not help thinking of a washerwoman. She played the final parting in such a way as to deprive it of all true tragic feeling, of which, indeed, the French have no notion at all. The same part was incomparably better played by the Italian Ristori; and, in fact, the Italian nature, though in many respects very different from the German, shares its appreciation for what is deep, serious, and true in Art; herein opposed to the French, which everywhere betrays that it possesses none of this feeling whatever.

The noble, in other words, the uncommon, element in the drama—nay, what is sublime in it—is not reached until the intellect is set to work, as opposed to the will; until it takes a free flight over all those passionate movements of the will, and makes them subject of its contemplation. Shakespeare, in particular, shows that this is his general method, more especially in Hamlet. And only when intellect rises to the point where the vanity of all effort is manifest, and the will proceeds to an act of self-annulment, is the drama tragic in the true sense of the word; it is then that it reaches its highest aim in becoming really sublime.

Every man takes the limits of his own field of vision for the limits of the world. This is an error of the intellect as inevitable as that error of the eye which lets us fancy that on the horizon heaven and earth meet. This explains many things, and among them the fact that everyone measures us with his own standard—generally about as long as a tailor's tape, and we have to put up with it: as also that no one will allow us to be taller than himself—a supposition which is once for all taken for granted.

There is no doubt that many a man owes his good fortune in life solely to the circumstance that he has a pleasant way of smiling, and so wins the heart in his favor.

However, the heart would do better to be careful, and to remember what Hamlet put down in his tablets—that one may smile, and smile, and be a villain.

Everything that is really fundamental in a man, and therefore genuine works, as such, unconsciously; in this respect like the power of nature. That which has passed through the domain of consciousness is thereby transformed into an idea or picture; and so if it comes to be uttered, it is only an idea or picture which passes from one person to another.

Accordingly, any quality of mind or character that is genuine and lasting, is originally unconscious; and it is only when unconsciously brought into play that it makes a profound impression. If any like quality is consciously exercised, it means that it has been worked up; it becomes intentional, and therefore matter of affectation, in other words, of deception.

If a man does a thing unconsciously, it costs him no trouble; but if he tries to do it by taking trouble, he fails. This applies to the origin of those fundamental ideas which form the pith and marrow of all genuine work. Only that which is innate is genuine and will hold water; and every man who wants to achieve something, whether in practical life, in literature, or in art, must follow the rules without knowing them.

Men of very great capacity, will as a rule, find the company of very stupid people preferable to that of the common run; for the same reason that the tyrant and the mob, the grandfather and the grandchildren, are natural allies.

That line of Ovid's,

Pronaque cum spectent animalia cetera terram,

can be applied in its true physical sense to the lower animals alone; but in a metaphorical and spiritual sense it is, alas! true of nearly all men as well. All their plans and projects are merged in the desire of physical enjoyment, physical well-being. They may, indeed, have personal interests, often embracing a very varied sphere; but still these latter receive their importance entirely from the relation in which they stand to the former. This is not only proved by their manner of life and the things they say, but it even shows itself in the way they look, the expression of their physiognomy, their gait and gesticulations. Everything about them cries out; in terram prona!

It is not to them, it is only to the nobler and more highly endowed natures—men who really think and look about them in the world, and form exceptional specimens of humanity—that the next lines are applicable;

Os homini sublime dedit coelumque tueri Jussit et erectos ad sidera tollere vultus.

No one knows what capacities for doing and suffering he has in himself, until something comes to rouse them to activity: just as in a pond of still water, lying there like a mirror, there is no sign of the roar and thunder with which it can leap from the precipice, and yet remain what it is; or again, rise high in the air as a fountain. When water is as cold as ice, you can have no idea of the latent warmth contained in it.

Why is it that, in spite of all the mirrors in the world, no one really knows what he looks like?

A man may call to mind the face of his friend, but not his own. Here, then, is an initial difficulty in the way of applying the maxim, Know thyself.

This is partly, no doubt, to be explained by the fact that it is physically impossible for a man to see himself in the glass except with face turned straight towards it and perfectly motionless; where the expression of the eye, which counts for so much, and really gives its whole character to the face, is to a great extent lost. But co-existing with this physical impossibility, there seems to me to be an ethical impossibility of an analogous nature, and producing the same effect. A man cannot look upon his own reflection as though the person presented there were a stranger to him; and yet this is necessary if he is to take an objective view. In the last resort, an objective view means a deep-rooted feeling on the part of the individual, as a moral being, that that which he is contemplating is not himself; and unless he can take this point of view, he will not see things in a really true light, which is possible only if he is alive to their actual defects, exactly as they are. Instead of that, when a man sees himself in the glass, something out of his own egotistic nature whispers to him to take care to remember that it is no stranger, but himself, that he is looking at; and this operates as a noli me tang ere, and prevents him taking an objective view. It seems, indeed, as if, without the leaven of a grain of malice, such a view were impossible.

According as a man's mental energy is exerted or relaxed, will life appear to him either so short, and petty, and fleeting, that nothing can possibly happen over which it is worth his while to spend emotion; that nothing really matters, whether it is pleasure or riches, or even fame, and that in whatever way a man may have failed, he cannot have lost much—or, on the other hand, life will seem so long, so important, so all in all, so momentous and so full of difficulty that we have to plunge into it with our whole soul if we are to obtain a share of its goods, make sure of its prizes, and carry out our plans. This latter is the immanent and common view of life; it is what Gracian means when he speaks of the serious way of looking at things—tomar muy de veras el vivir. The former is the transcendental view, which is well expressed in Ovid's non est tanti—it is not worth so much trouble; still better, however, by Plato's remark that nothing in human affairs is worth any great anxiety—[Greek: oute ti ton anthropinon axion esti megalaes spoudaes.] This condition of mind is due to the intellect having got the upper hand in the domain of consciousness, where, freed from the mere service of the will, it looks upon the phenomena of life objectively, and so cannot fail to gain a clear insight into its vain and futile character. But in the other condition of mind, will predominates; and the intellect exists only to light it on its way to the attainment of its desires.

A man is great or small according as he leans to the one or the other of these views of life.

People of very brilliant ability think little of admitting their errors and weaknesses, or of letting others see them. They look upon them as something for which they have duly paid; and instead of fancying that these weaknesses are a disgrace to them, they consider they are doing them an honor. This is especially the case when the errors are of the kind that hang together with their qualities—conditiones sine quibus non—or, as George Sand said, les défauts de ses vertus.

Contrarily, there are people of good character and irreproachable intellectual capacity, who, far from admitting the few little weaknesses they have, conceal them with care, and show themselves very sensitive to any suggestion of their existence; and this, just because their whole merit consists in being free from error and infirmity. If these people are found to have done anything wrong, their reputation immediately suffers.

With people of only moderate ability, modesty is mere honesty; but with those who possess great talent, it is hypocrisy. Hence, it is just as becoming in the latter to make no secret of the respect they bear themselves and no disguise of the fact that they are conscious of unusual power, as it is in the former to be modest. Valerius Maximus gives some very neat examples of this in his chapter on self-confidence, de fiducia sui.

Not to go to the theatre is like making one's toilet without a mirror. But it is still worse to take a decision without consulting a friend. For a man may have the most excellent judgment in all other matters, and yet go wrong in those which concern himself; because here the will comes in and deranges the intellect at once. Therefore let a man take counsel of a friend. A doctor can cure everyone but himself; if he falls ill, he sends for a colleague.

In all that we do, we wish, more or less, to come to the end; we are impatient to finish and glad to be done. But the last scene of all, the general end, is something that, as a rule, we wish as far off as may be.

Every parting gives a foretaste of death; every coming together again a foretaste of the resurrection. This is why even people who were indifferent to each other, rejoice so much if they come together again after twenty or thirty years' separation.

Intellects differ from one another in a very real and fundamental way: but no comparison can well be made by merely general observations. It is necessary to come close, and to go into details; for the difference that exists cannot be seen from afar; and it is not easy to judge by outward appearances, as in the several cases of education, leisure and occupation. But even judging by these alone, it must be admitted that many a man has a degree of existence at least ten times as high as another—in other words, exists ten times as much.

I am not speaking here of savages whose life is often only one degree above that of the apes in their woods. Consider, for instance, a porter in Naples or Venice (in the north of Europe solicitude for the winter months makes people more thoughtful and therefore reflective); look at the life he leads, from its beginning to its end:—driven by poverty; living on his physical strength; meeting the needs of every day, nay, of every hour, by hard work, great effort, constant tumult, want in all its forms, no care for the morrow; his only comfort rest after exhaustion; continuous quarreling; not a moment free for reflection; such sensual delights as a mild climate and only just sufficient food will permit of; and then, finally, as the metaphysical element, the crass superstition of his church; the whole forming a manner of life with only a low degree of consciousness, where a man hustles, or rather is hustled, through his existence. This restless and confused dream forms the life of how many millions!

Such men think only just so much as is necessary to carry out their will for the moment. They never reflect upon their life as a connected whole, let alone, then, upon existence in general; to a certain extent they may be said to exist without really knowing it. The existence of the mobsman or the slave who lives on in this unthinking way, stands very much nearer than ours to that of the brute, which is confined entirely to the present moment; but, for that very reason, it has also less of pain in it than ours. Nay, since all pleasure is in its nature negative, that is to say, consists in freedom from some form of misery or need, the constant and rapid interchange between setting about something and getting it done, which is the permanent accompaniment of the work they do, and then again the augmented form which this takes when they go from work to rest and the satisfaction of their needs—all this gives them a constant source of enjoyment; and the fact that it is much commoner to see happy faces amongst the poor than amongst the rich, is a sure proof that it is used to good advantage.

Passing from this kind of man, consider, next, the sober, sensible merchant, who leads a life of speculation, thinks long over his plans and carries them out with great care, founds a house, and provides for his wife, his children and descendants; takes his share, too, in the life of a community. It is obvious that a man like this has a much higher degree of consciousness than the former, and so his existence has a higher degree of reality.

Then look at the man of learning, who investigates, it may be, the history of the past. He will have reached the point at which a man becomes conscious of existence as a whole, sees beyond the period of his own life, beyond his own personal interests, thinking over the whole course of the world's history.

Then, finally, look at the poet or the philosopher, in whom reflection has reached such a height, that, instead of being drawn on to investigate any one particular phenomenon of existence, he stands in amazement before existence itself, this great sphinx, and makes it his problem. In him consciousness has reached the degree of clearness at which it embraces the world itself: his intellect has completely abandoned its function as the servant of his will, and now holds the world before him; and the world calls upon him much more to examine and consider it, than to play a part in it himself. If, then, the degree of consciousness is the degree of reality, such a man will be said to exist most of all, and there will be sense and significance in so describing him.

Between the two extremes here sketched, and the intervening stages, everyone will be able to find the place at which he himself stands.

We know that man is in general superior to all other animals, and this is also the case in his capacity for being trained. Mohammedans are trained to pray with their faces turned towards Mecca, five times a day; and they never fail to do it. Christians are trained to cross themselves on certain occasions, to bow, and so on. Indeed, it may be said that religion is the chef d'oeuvre of the art of training, because it trains people in the way they shall think: and, as is well known, you cannot begin the process too early. There is no absurdity so palpable but that it may be firmly planted in the human head if you only begin to inculcate it before the age of five, by constantly repeating it with an air of great solemnity. For as in the case of animals, so in that of men, training is successful only when you begin in early youth.

Noblemen and gentlemen are trained to hold nothing sacred but their word of honor—to maintain a zealous, rigid, and unshaken belief in the ridiculous code of chivalry; and if they are called upon to do so, to seal their belief by dying for it, and seriously to regard a king as a being of a higher order.

Again, our expressions of politeness, the compliments we make, in particular, the respectful attentions we pay to ladies, are a matter of training; as also our esteem for good birth, rank, titles, and so on. Of the same character is the resentment we feel at any insult directed against us; and the measure of this resentment may be exactly determined by the nature of the insult. An Englishman, for instance, thinks it a deadly insult to be told that he is no gentleman, or, still worse, that he is a liar; a Frenchman has the same feeling if you call him a coward, and a German if you say he is stupid.

There are many persons who are trained to be strictly honorable in regard to one particular matter, while they have little honor to boast of in anything else. Many a man, for instance, will not steal your money; but he will lay hands on everything of yours that he can enjoy without having to pay for it. A man of business will often deceive you without the slightest scruple, but he will absolutely refuse to commit a theft.

Imagination is strong in a man when that particular function of the brain which enables him to observe is roused to activity without any necessary excitement of the senses. Accordingly, we find that imagination is active just in proportion as our senses are not excited by external objects. A long period of solitude, whether in prison or in a sick room; quiet, twilight, darkness—these are the things that promote its activity; and under their influence it comes into play of itself. On the other hand, when a great deal of material is presented to our faculties of observation, as happens on a journey, or in the hurly-burly of the world, or, again, in broad daylight, the imagination is idle, and, even though call may be made upon it, refuses to become active, as though it understood that that was not its proper time.

However, if the imagination is to yield any real product, it must have received a great deal of material from the external world. This is the only way in which its storehouse can be filled. The phantasy is nourished much in the same way as the body, which is least capable of any work and enjoys doing nothing just in the very moment when it receives its food which it has to digest. And yet it is to this very food that it owes the power which it afterwards puts forth at the right time.

Opinion is like a pendulum and obeys the same law. If it goes past the centre of gravity on one side, it must go a like distance on the other; and it is only after a certain time that it finds the true point at which it can remain at rest.

By a process of contradiction, distance in space makes things look small, and therefore free from defect. This is why a landscape looks so much better in a contracting mirror or in a camera obscura, than it is in reality. The same effect is produced by distance in time. The scenes and events of long ago, and the persons who took part in them, wear a charming aspect to the eye of memory, which sees only the outlines and takes no note of disagreeable details. The present enjoys no such advantage, and so it always seems defective.

And again, as regards space, small objects close to us look big, and if they are very close, we may be able to see nothing else, but when we go a little way off, they become minute and invisible. It is the same again as regards time. The little incidents and accidents of every day fill us with emotion, anxiety, annoyance, passion, as long as they are close to us, when they appear so big, so important, so serious; but as soon as they are borne down the restless stream of time, they lose what significance they had; we think no more of them and soon forget them altogether. They were big only because they were near.

Joy and sorrow are not ideas of the mind, but affections of the will, and so they do not lie in the domain of memory. We cannot recall our joys and sorrows; by which I mean that we cannot renew them. We can recall only the ideas that accompanied them; and, in particular, the things we were led to say; and these form a gauge of our feelings at the time. Hence our memory of joys and sorrows is always imperfect, and they become a matter of indifference to us as soon as they are over. This explains the vanity of the attempt, which we sometimes make, to revive the pleasures and the pains of the past. Pleasure and pain are essentially an affair of the will; and the will, as such, is not possessed of memory, which is a function of the intellect; and this in its turn gives out and takes in nothing but thoughts and ideas, which are not here in question.

It is a curious fact that in bad days we can very vividly recall the good time that is now no more; but that in good days, we have only a very cold and imperfect memory of the bad.

We have a much better memory of actual objects or pictures than for mere ideas. Hence a good imagination makes it easier to learn languages; for by its aid, the new word is at once united with the actual object to which it refers; whereas, if there is no imagination, it is simply put on a parallel with the equivalent word in the mother tongue.

Mnemonics should not only mean the art of keeping something indirectly in the memory by the use of some direct pun or witticism; it should, rather, be applied to a systematic theory of memory, and explain its several attributes by reference both to its real nature, and to the relation in which these attributes stand to one another.

There are moments in life when our senses obtain a higher and rarer degree of clearness, apart from any particular occasion for it in the nature of our surroundings; and explicable, rather, on physiological grounds alone, as the result of some enhanced state of susceptibility, working from within outwards. Such moments remain indelibly impressed upon the memory, and preserve themselves in their individuality entire. We can assign no reason for it, nor explain why this among so many thousand moments like it should be specially remembered. It seems as much a matter of chance as when single specimens of a whole race of animals now extinct are discovered in the layers of a rock; or when, on opening a book, we light upon an insect accidentally crushed within the leaves. Memories of this kind are always sweet and pleasant.

It occasionally happens that, for no particular reason, long-forgotten scenes suddenly start up in the memory. This may in many cases be due to the action of some hardly perceptible odor, which accompanied those scenes and now recurs exactly same as before. For it is well known that the sense of smell is specially effective in awakening memories, and that in general it does not require much to rouse a train of ideas. And I may say, in passing, that the sense of sight is connected with the understanding, the sense of hearing with the reason,[2] and, as we see in the present case, the sense of smell with the memory. Touch and Taste are more material and dependent upon contact. They have no ideal side.

It must also be reckoned among the peculiar attributes of memory that a slight state of intoxication often so greatly enhances the recollection of past times and scenes, that all the circumstances connected with them come back much more clearly than would be possible in a state of sobriety; but that, on the other hand, the recollection of what one said or did while the intoxication lasted, is more than usually imperfect; nay, that if one has been absolutely tipsy, it is gone altogether. We may say, then, that whilst intoxication enhances the memory for what is past, it allows it to remember little of the present.

Men need some kind of external activity, because they are inactive within. Contrarily, if they are active within, they do not care to be dragged out of themselves; it disturbs and impedes their thoughts in a way that is often most ruinous to them.

I am not surprised that some people are bored when they find themselves alone; for they cannot laugh if they are quite by themselves. The very idea of it seems folly to them.

Are we, then, to look upon laughter as merely O signal for others — a mere sign, like a word? What makes it impossible for people to laugh when they are alone is nothing but want of imagination, dullness of mind generally — [Greek: anaisthaesia kai bradutaes psuchaes], as Theophrastus has it. The lower animals never laugh, either alone or in company. Myson, the misanthropist, was once surprised by one of these people as he was laughing to himself. Why do you laugh? he asked; there is no one with you. That is just why I am laughing, said Myson.

Natural gesticulation, such as commonly accompanies any lively talk, is a language of its own, more widespread, even, than the language of words—so far, I mean, as it is independent of words and alike in all nations. It is true that nations make use of it in proportion as they are vivacious, and that in particular cases, amongst the Italians, for instance, it is supplemented by certain peculiar gestures which are merely conventional, and therefore possessed of nothing more than a local value.

In the universal use made of it, gesticulation has some analogy with logic and grammar, in that it has to do with the form, rather than with the matter of conversation; but on the other hand it is distinguishable from them by the fact that it has more of a moral than of an intellectual bearing; in other words, it reflects the movements of the will. As an accompaniment of conversation it is like the bass of a melody; and if, as in music, it keeps true to the progress of the treble, it serves to heighten the effect.

In a conversation, the gesture depends upon the form in which the subject-matter is conveyed; and it is interesting to observe that, whatever that subject-matter may be, with a recurrence of the form, the very same gesture is repeated. So if I happen to see—from my window, say—two persons carrying on a lively conversation, without my being able to catch a word, I can, nevertheless, understand the general nature of it perfectly well; I mean, the kind of thing that is being said and the form it takes. There is no mistake about it. The speaker is arguing about something, advancing his reasons, then limiting their application, then driving them home and drawing the conclusion in triumph; or he is recounting his experiences, proving, perhaps, beyond the shadow of a doubt, how much he has been injured, but bringing the clearest and most damning evidence to show that his opponents were foolish and obstinate people who would not be convinced; or else he is telling of the splendid plan he laid, and how he carried it to a successful issue, or perhaps failed because the luck was against him; or, it may be, he is saying that he was completely at a loss to know what to do, or that he was quick in seeing some traps set for him, and that by insisting on his rights or by applying a little force, he succeeded in frustrating and punishing his enemies; and so on in hundreds of cases of a similar kind.

Strictly speaking, however, what I get from gesticulation alone is an abstract notion of the essential drift of what is being said, and that, too, whether I judge from a moral or an intellectual point of view. It is the quintessence, the true substance of the conversation, and this remains identical, no matter what may have given rise to the conversation, or what it may be about; the relation between the two being that of a general idea or class-name to the individuals which it covers.

As I have said, the most interesting and amusing part of the matter is the complete identity and solidarity of the gestures used to denote the same set of circumstances, even though by people of very different temperament; so that the gestures become exactly like words of a language, alike for every one, and subject only to such small modifications as depend upon variety of accent and education. And yet there can be no doubt but that these standing gestures, which every one uses, are the result of no convention or collusion. They are original and innate—a true language of nature; consolidated, it may be, by imitation and the influence of custom.

It is well known that it is part of an actor's duty to make a careful study of gesture; and the same thing is true, to a somewhat smaller degree, of a public speaker. This study must consist chiefly in watching others and imitating their movements, for there are no abstract rules fairly applicable to the matter, with the exception of some very general leading principles, such as—to take an example—that the gesture must not follow the word, but rather come immediately before it, by way of announcing its approach and attracting the hearer's attention.

Englishmen entertain a peculiar contempt for gesticulation, and look upon it as something vulgar and undignified. This seems to me a silly prejudice on their part, and the outcome of their general prudery. For here we have a language which nature has given to every one, and which every one understands; and to do away with and forbid it for no better reason than that it is opposed to that much-lauded thing, gentlemanly feeling, is a very questionable proceeding.

ON EDUCATION.

The human intellect is said to be so constituted that general ideas arise by abstraction from particular observations, and therefore come after them in point of time. If this is what actually occurs, as happens in the case of a man who has to depend solely upon his own experience for what he learns—who has no teacher and no book,—such a man knows quite well which of his particular observations belong to and are represented by each of his general ideas. He has a perfect acquaintance with both sides of his experience, and accordingly, he treats everything that comes in his way from a right standpoint. This might be called the natural method of education.

Contrarily, the artificial method is to hear what other people say, to learn and to read, and so to get your head crammed full of general ideas before you have any sort of extended acquaintance with the world as it is, and as you may see it for yourself. You will be told that the particular observations which go to make these general ideas will come to you later on in the course of experience; but until that time arrives, you apply your general ideas wrongly, you judge men and things from a wrong standpoint, you see them in a wrong light, and treat them in a wrong way. So it is that education perverts the mind.

This explains why it so frequently happens that, after a long course of learning and reading, we enter upon the world in our youth, partly with an artless ignorance of things, partly with wrong notions about them; so that our demeanor savors at one moment of a nervous anxiety, at another of a mistaken confidence. The reason of this is simply that our head is full of general ideas which we are now trying to turn to some use, but which we hardly ever apply rightly. This is the result of acting in direct opposition to the natural development of the mind by obtaining general ideas first, and particular observations last: it is putting the cart before the horse. Instead of developing the child's own faculties of discernment, and teaching it to judge and think for itself, the teacher uses all his energies to stuff its head full of the ready-made thoughts of other people. The mistaken views of life, which spring from a false application of general ideas, have afterwards to be corrected by long years of experience; and it is seldom that they are wholly corrected. This is why so few men of learning are possessed of common-sense, such as is often to be met with in people who have had no instruction at all.

To acquire a knowledge of the world might be defined as the aim of all education; and it follows from what I have said that special stress should be laid upon beginning to acquire this knowledge at the right end. As I have shown, this means, in the main, that the particular observation of a thing shall precede the general idea of it; further, that narrow and circumscribed ideas shall come before ideas of a wide range. It means, therefore, that the whole system of education shall follow in the steps that must have been taken by the ideas themselves in the course of their formation. But whenever any of these steps are skipped or left out, the instruction is defective, and the ideas obtained are false; and finally, a distorted view of the world arises, peculiar to the individual himself—a view such as almost everyone entertains for some time, and most men for as long as they live. No one can look into his own mind without seeing that it was only after reaching a very mature age, and in some cases when he least expected it, that he came to a right understanding or a clear view of many matters in his life, that, after all, were not very difficult or complicated. Up till then, they were points in his knowledge of the world which were still obscure, due to his having skipped some particular lesson in those early days of his education, whatever it may have been like—whether artificial and conventional, or of that natural kind which is based upon individual experience.

It follows that an attempt should be made to find out the strictly natural course of knowledge, so that education may proceed methodically by keeping to it; and that children may become acquainted with the ways of the world, without getting wrong ideas into their heads, which very often cannot be got out again. If this plan were adopted, special care would have to be taken to prevent children from using words without clearly understanding their meaning and application. The fatal tendency to be satisfied with words instead of trying to understand things—to learn phrases by heart, so that they may prove a refuge in time of need, exists, as a rule, even in children; and the tendency lasts on into manhood, making the knowledge of many learned persons to consist in mere verbiage.

However, the main endeavor must always be to let particular observations precede general ideas, and not vice versa, as is usually and unfortunately the case; as though a child should come feet foremost into the world, or a verse be begun by writing down the rhyme! The ordinary method is to imprint ideas and opinions, in the strict sense of the word, prejudices, on the mind of the child, before it has had any but a very few particular observations. It is thus that he afterwards comes to view the world and gather experience through the medium of those ready-made ideas, rather than to let his ideas be formed for him out of his own experience of life, as they ought to be.

A man sees a great many things when he looks at the world for himself, and he sees them from many sides; but this method of learning is not nearly so short or so quick as the method which employs abstract ideas and makes hasty generalizations about everything. Experience, therefore, will be a long time in correcting preconceived ideas, or perhaps never bring its task to an end; for wherever a man finds that the aspect of things seems to contradict the general ideas he has formed, he will begin by rejecting the evidence it offers as partial and one-sided; nay, he will shut his eyes to it altogether and deny that it stands in any contradiction at all with his preconceived notions, in order that he may thus preserve them uninjured. So it is that many a man carries about a burden of wrong notions all his life long—crotchets, whims, fancies, prejudices, which at last become fixed ideas. The fact is that he has never tried to form his fundamental ideas for himself out of his own experience of life, his own way of looking at the world, because he has taken over his ideas ready-made from other people; and this it is that makes him—as it makes how many others!—so shallow and superficial.

Instead of that method of instruction, care should be taken to educate children on the natural lines. No idea should ever be established in a child's mind otherwise than by what the child can see for itself, or at any rate it should be verified by the same means; and the result of this would be that the child's ideas, if few, would be well-grounded and accurate. It would learn how to measure things by its own standard rather than by another's; and so it would escape a thousand strange fancies and prejudices, and not need to have them eradicated by the lessons it will subsequently be taught in the school of life. The child would, in this way, have its mind once for all habituated to clear views and thorough-going knowledge; it would use its own judgment and take an unbiased estimate of things.

And, in general, children should not form their notions of what life is like from the copy before they have learned it from the original, to whatever aspect of it their attention may be directed. Instead, therefore, of hastening to place books, and books alone, in their hands, let them be made acquainted, step by step, with things—with the actual circumstances of human life. And above all let care be taken to bring them to a clear and objective view of the world as it is, to educate them always to derive their ideas directly from real life, and to shape them in conformity with it—not to fetch them from other sources, such as books, fairy tales, or what people say—then to apply them ready-made to real life. For this will mean that their heads are full of wrong notions, and that they will either see things in a false light or try in vain to remodel the world to suit their views, and so enter upon false paths; and that, too, whether they are only constructing theories of life or engaged in the actual business of it. It is incredible how much harm is done when the seeds of wrong notions are laid in the mind in those early years, later on to bear a crop of prejudice; for the subsequent lessons, which are learned from real life in the world have to be devoted mainly to their extirpation. To unlearn the evil was the answer, according to Diogenes Laertius, Antisthenes gave, when he was asked what branch of knowledge was most necessary; and we can see what he meant.

No child under the age of fifteen should receive instruction in subjects which may possibly be the vehicle of serious error, such as philosophy, religion, or any other branch of knowledge where it is necessary to take large views; because wrong notions imbibed early can seldom be rooted out, and of all the intellectual faculties, judgment is the last to arrive at maturity. The child should give its attention either to subjects where no error is possible at all, such as mathematics, or to those in which there is no particular danger in making a mistake, such as languages, natural science, history and so on. And in general, the branches of knowledge which are to be studied at any period of life should be such as the mind is equal to at that period and can perfectly understand. Childhood and youth form the time for collecting materials, for getting a special and thorough knowledge of the individual and particular things. In those years it is too early to form views on a large scale; and ultimate explanations must be put off to a later date. The faculty of judgment, which cannot come into play without mature experience, should be left to itself; and care should be taken not to anticipate its action by inculcating prejudice, which will paralyze it for ever.

On the other hand, the memory should be specially taxed in youth, since it is then that it is strongest and most tenacious. But in choosing the things that should be committed to memory the utmost care and forethought must be exercised; as lessons well learnt in youth are never forgotten. This precious soil must therefore be cultivated so as to bear as much fruit as possible. If you think how deeply rooted in your memory are those persons whom you knew in the first twelve years of your life, how indelible the impression made upon you by the events of those years, how clear your recollection of most of the things that happened to you then, most of what was told or taught you, it will seem a natural thing to take the susceptibility and tenacity of the mind at that period as the ground-work of education. This may be done by a strict observance of method, and a systematic regulation of the impressions which the mind is to receive.

But the years of youth allotted to a man are short, and memory is, in general, bound within narrow limits; still more so, the memory of any one individual. Since this is the case, it is all-important to fill the memory with what is essential and material in any branch of knowledge, to the exclusion of everything else. The decision as to what is essential and material should rest with the masterminds in every department of thought; their choice should be made after the most mature deliberation, and the outcome of it fixed and determined. Such a choice would have to proceed by sifting the things which it is necessary and important for a man to know in general, and then, necessary and important for him to know in any particular business or calling. Knowledge of the first kind would have to be classified, after an encyclopaedic fashion, in graduated courses, adapted to the degree of general culture which a man may be expected to have in the circumstances in which he is placed; beginning with a course limited to the necessary requirements of primary education, and extending upwards to the subjects treated of in all the branches of philosophical thought. The regulation of the second kind of knowledge would be left to those who had shown genuine mastery in the several departments into which it is divided; and the whole system would provide an elaborate rule or canon for intellectual education, which would, of course, have to be revised every ten years. Some such arrangement as this would employ the youthful power of the memory to best advantage, and supply excellent working material to the faculty of judgment, when it made its appearance later on.

A man's knowledge may be said to be mature, in other words, it has reached the most complete state of perfection to which he, as an individual, is capable of bringing it, when an exact correspondence is established between the whole of his abstract ideas and the things he has actually perceived for himself. This will mean that each of his abstract ideas rests, directly or indirectly, upon a basis of observation, which alone endows it with any real value; and also that he is able to place every observation he makes under the right abstract idea which belongs to it. Maturity is the work of experience alone; and therefore it requires time. The knowledge we derive from our own observation is usually distinct from that which we acquire through the medium of abstract ideas; the one coming to us in the natural way, the other by what people tell us, and the course of instruction we receive, whether it is good or bad. The result is, that in youth there is generally very little agreement or correspondence between our abstract ideas, which are merely phrases in the mind, and that real knowledge which we have obtained by our own observation. It is only later on that a gradual approach takes place between these two kinds of knowledge, accompanied by a mutual correction of error; and knowledge is not mature until this coalition is accomplished. This maturity or perfection of knowledge is something quite independent of another kind of perfection, which may be of a high or a low order—the perfection, I mean, to which a man may bring his own individual faculties; which is measured, not by any correspondence between the two kinds of knowledge, but by the degree of intensity which each kind attains.

For the practical man the most needful thing is to acquire an accurate and profound knowledge of the ways of the world. But this, though the most needful, is also the most wearisome of all studies, as a man may reach a great age without coming to the end of his task; whereas, in the domain of the sciences, he masters the more important facts when he is still young. In acquiring that knowledge of the world, it is while he is a novice, namely, in boyhood and in youth, that the first and hardest lessons are put before him; but it often happens that even in later years there is still a great deal to be learned.

The study is difficult enough in itself; but the difficulty is doubled by novels, which represent a state of things in life and the world, such as, in fact, does not exist. Youth is credulous, and accepts these views of life, which then become part and parcel of the mind; so that, instead of a merely negative condition of ignorance, you have positive error—a whole tissue of false notions to start with; and at a later date these actually spoil the schooling of experience, and put a wrong construction on the lessons it teaches. If, before this, the youth had no light at all to guide him, he is now misled by a will-o'-the-wisp; still more often is this the case with a girl. They have both had a false view of things foisted on them by reading novels; and expectations have been aroused which can never be fulfilled. This generally exercises a baneful influence on their whole life. In this respect those whose youth has allowed them no time or opportunity for reading novels—those who work with their hands and the like—are in a position of decided advantage. There are a few novels to which this reproach cannot be addressed—nay, which have an effect the contrary of bad. First and foremost, to give an example, Gil Blas, and the other works of Le Sage (or rather their Spanish originals); further, The Vicar of

Wakefield, and, to some extent Sir Walter Scott's novels. Don Quixote may be regarded as a satirical exhibition of the error to which I am referring.

OF WOMEN.

Schiller's poem in honor of women, Würde der Frauen, is the result of much careful thought, and it appeals to the reader by its antithetic style and its use of contrast; but as an expression of the true praise which should be accorded to them, it is, I think, inferior to these few words of Jouy's: Without women, the beginning of our life would be helpless; the middle, devoid of pleasure; and the end, of consolation. The same thing is more feelingly expressed by Byron in Sardanapalus:

> The very first
> Of human life must spring from woman's breast,
> Your first small words are taught you from her lips,
> Your first tears quench'd by her, and your last sighs
> Too often breathed out in a woman's hearing,
> When men have shrunk from the ignoble care
> Of watching the last hour of him who led them.

(Act I Scene 2.)

These two passages indicate the right standpoint for the appreciation of women.

You need only look at the way in which she is formed, to see that woman is not meant to undergo great labor, whether of the mind or of the body. She pays the debt of life not by what she does, but by what she suffers; by the pains of child-bearing and care for the child, and by submission to her husband, to whom she should be a patient and cheering companion. The keenest sorrows and joys are not for her, nor is she called upon to display a great deal of strength. The current of her life should be more gentle, peaceful and trivial than man's, without being essentially happier or unhappier.

Women are directly fitted for acting as the nurses and teachers of our early childhood by the fact that they are themselves childish, frivolous and short-sighted; in a word, they are big children all their life long—a kind of intermediate stage between the child and the full-grown man, who is man in the strict sense of the word. See how a girl will fondle a child for days together, dance with it and sing to it; and then think what a man, with the best will in the world, could do if he were put in her place.

With young girls Nature seems to have had in view what, in the language of the drama, is called a striking effect; as for a few years she dowers them with a wealth of beauty and is lavish in her gift of charm, at the expense of all the rest of their life; so that during those years they may capture the fantasy of some man to such a degree that he is hurried away into undertaking the honorable care of them, in some form or other, as long as they live—a step for which there would not appear to be any sufficient warranty if reason only directed his thoughts. Accordingly, Nature has equipped woman, as she does all her creatures, with the weapons and implements requisite for the safeguarding of her existence, and for just as long as it is necessary for her to have them. Here, as elsewhere, Nature proceeds with her usual economy; for just as the female ant, after fecundation, loses her wings, which are then superfluous, nay, actually a danger to the business of breeding; so, after giving birth to one or two children, a woman generally loses her beauty; probably, indeed, for similar reasons.

And so we find that young girls, in their hearts, look upon domestic affairs or work of any kind as of secondary importance, if not actually as a mere jest. The only business that really claims their earnest attention is love, making conquests, and everything connected with this—dress, dancing, and so on.

The nobler and more perfect a thing is, the later and slower it is in arriving at maturity. A man reaches the maturity of his reasoning powers and mental faculties hardly before the age of twenty-eight; a woman at eighteen. And then, too, in the case of woman, it is only reason of a sort—very niggard in its dimensions. That is why women remain children their whole life long; never seeing anything but what is quite close to them, cleaving to the present moment, taking appearance for reality, and preferring trifles to matters of the first importance. For it is by virtue of his reasoning faculty that man does not live in the present only, like the brute, but looks about him and considers the past and the future; and this is the origin of prudence, as well as of that care and anxiety which so many people exhibit. Both the advantages and the disadvantages which this involves, are shared in by the woman to a smaller extent because of her weaker power of reasoning. She may, in fact, be described as intellectually short-sighted, because, while she has an intuitive understanding of what lies quite close to her, her field of vision is narrow and does not reach to what is remote; so that things which are absent, or past, or to come, have much less effect upon women than upon men. This is the reason why women are more often inclined to be extravagant, and sometimes carry their inclination to a length that borders upon madness. In their hearts, women think that it is men's business to earn money and theirs to spend it—- if possible during their husband's life, but, at any rate, after his death. The very fact that their husband hands them over his earnings for purposes of housekeeping, strengthens them in this belief.

However many disadvantages all this may involve, there is at least this to be said in its favor; that the woman lives more in the present than the man, and that, if the present is at all tolerable, she enjoys it more eagerly. This is the source of that cheerfulness which is peculiar to women, fitting her to amuse man in his hours of recreation, and, in case of need, to console him when he is borne down by the weight of his cares.

It is by no means a bad plan to consult women in matters of difficulty, as the Germans used to do in ancient times; for their way of looking at things is quite different from ours, chiefly in the fact that they like to take the shortest way to their goal, and, in general, manage to fix their eyes upon what lies before them; while we, as a rule, see far beyond it, just because it is in front of our noses. In cases like this, we need to be brought back to the right standpoint, so as to recover the near and simple view.

Then, again, women are decidedly more sober in their judgment than we are, so that they do not see more in things than is really there; whilst, if our passions are aroused, we are apt to see things in an exaggerated way, or imagine what does not exist.

The weakness of their reasoning faculty also explains why it is that women show more sympathy for the unfortunate than men do, and so treat them with more kindness and interest; and why it is that, on the contrary, they are inferior to men in point of justice, and less honorable and conscientious. For it is just because their reasoning power is weak that present circumstances have such a hold over them, and those concrete things, which lie directly before their eyes, exercise a power which is seldom counteracted to any extent by abstract principles of thought, by fixed rules of conduct, firm resolutions, or, in general, by consideration for the past and the future, or regard for what is absent and remote. Accordingly, they possess the first and main elements that go to make a virtuous character, but they are deficient in those secondary qualities which are often a necessary instrument in the formation of it.

Hence, it will be found that the fundamental fault of the female character is that it has no sense of justice. This is mainly due to the fact, already mentioned, that women are defective in the powers of reasoning and deliberation; but it is also traceable to the position which Nature has assigned to them as the weaker sex. They are dependent, not upon strength, but upon craft; and hence their instinctive capacity for cunning, and their ineradicable tendency to say what is not true. For as lions are provided with claws and teeth, and elephants and boars with tusks, bulls with horns, and cuttle fish with its clouds of inky fluid, so Nature has equipped woman, for her defence and protection, with the arts of dissimulation; and all the power which Nature has conferred upon man in the shape of physical strength and reason, has been bestowed upon women in this form. Hence, dissimulation is innate in woman, and almost as much a quality of the stupid as of the clever. It is as natural for them to make use of it on every occasion as it is for those animals to employ their means of defence when they are attacked; they have a feeling that in doing so they are only within their rights. Therefore a woman who is perfectly truthful and not given to dissimulation is perhaps an impossibility, and for this very reason they are so quick at seeing through dissimulation in others that it is not a wise thing to attempt it with them. But this fundamental defect which I have stated, with all that it entails, gives rise to falsity, faithlessness, treachery, ingratitude, and so on. Perjury in a court of justice is more often committed by women than by men. It may, indeed, be generally questioned whether women ought to be sworn in at all. From time to time one finds repeated cases everywhere of ladies, who want for nothing, taking things from shop-counters when no one is looking, and making off with them.

Nature has appointed that the propagation of the species shall be the business of men who are young, strong and handsome; so that the race may not degenerate. This is the firm will and purpose of Nature in regard to the species, and it finds its expression in the passions of women. There is no law that is older or more powerful than this. Woe, then, to the man who sets up claims and interests that will conflict with it; whatever he may say and do, they will be unmercifully crushed at the first serious encounter. For the innate rule that governs women's conduct, though it is secret and unformulated, nay, unconscious in its working, is this: We are justified in deceiving those who think they have acquired rights over the species by paying little attention to the individual, that is, to us. The constitution and, therefore, the welfare of the species have been placed in our hands and committed to our care, through the control we obtain over the next generation, which proceeds from us; let us discharge our duties conscientiously. But women have no abstract knowledge of this leading principle; they are conscious of it only as a concrete fact; and they have no other method of giving expression to it than the way in which they act when the opportunity arrives. And then their conscience does not trouble them so much as we fancy; for in the darkest recesses of their heart, they are aware that in committing a breach of their duty towards the individual, they have all the better fulfilled their duty towards the species, which is infinitely greater.

And since women exist in the main solely for the propagation of the species, and are not destined for anything else, they live, as a rule, more for the species than for the individual, and in their hearts take the affairs of the species more seriously than those of the individual. This gives their whole life and being a certain levity; the general bent of their character is in a direction fundamentally different from that of man; and it is this to which produces that discord in married life which is so frequent, and almost the normal state.

The natural feeling between men is mere indifference, but between women it is actual enmity. The reason of this is that trade-jealousy—odium figulinum—which, in the case of men does not go beyond the confines of their own particular pursuit; but, with women, embraces the whole sex; since they have only one kind of business. Even when they meet in the street, women look at one another like Guelphs and Ghibellines. And it is a patent fact that when two women make first acquaintance with each other, they behave with more constraint and dissimulation than two men would show in a like case; and hence it is that an exchange of compliments between two women is a much more ridiculous proceeding than between two men. Further, whilst a man will, as a general rule, always preserve a certain amount of consideration and humanity in speaking to others, even to those who are in a very inferior position, it is intolerable to see how proudly and disdainfully a fine lady will generally behave towards one who is in a lower social rank (I do not mean a woman who is in her service), whenever she speaks to her. The reason of this may be that, with women, differences of rank are much more precarious than with us; because, while a hundred considerations carry weight in our case, in theirs there is only one, namely, with which man they have found favor; as also that they stand in much nearer relations with one another than men do, in consequence of the one-sided nature of their calling. This makes them endeavor to lay stress upon differences of rank.

It is only the man whose intellect is clouded by his sexual impulses that could give the name of the fair sex to that under-sized, narrow-shouldered, broad-hipped, and short-legged race; for the whole beauty of the sex is bound up with this impulse. Instead of calling them beautiful, there would be more warrant for describing women as the un-aesthetic sex. Neither for music, nor for poetry, nor for fine art, have they really and truly any sense or susceptibility; it is a mere mockery if they make a pretence of it in order to assist their endeavor to please. Hence, as a result of this, they are incapable of taking a purely objective interest in anything; and the reason of it seems to me to be as follows. A man tries to acquire direct mastery over things, either by understanding them, or by forcing them to do his will. But a woman is always and everywhere reduced to obtaining this mastery indirectly, namely, through a man; and whatever direct mastery she may have is entirely confined to him. And so it lies in woman's nature to look upon everything only as a means for conquering man; and if she takes an interest in anything else, it is simulated—a mere roundabout way of gaining her ends by coquetry, and feigning what she does not feel. Hence, even Rousseau declared: Women have, in general, no love for any art; they have no proper knowledge of any; and they have no genius.

No one who sees at all below the surface can have failed to remark the same thing. You need only observe the kind of attention women bestow upon a concert, an opera, or a play—the childish simplicity, for example, with which they keep on chattering during the finest passages in the greatest masterpieces. If it is true that the Greeks excluded women from their theatres they were quite right in what they did; at any rate you would have been able to hear what was said upon the stage. In our day, besides, or in lieu of saying, Let a woman keep silence in the church, it would be much to the point to say Let a woman keep silence in the theatre. This might, perhaps, be put up in big letters on the curtain.

And you cannot expect anything else of women if you consider that the most distinguished intellects among the whole sex have never managed to produce a single achievement in the fine arts that is really great, genuine, and original; or given to the world any work of permanent value in any sphere. This is most strikingly shown in regard to painting, where mastery of technique is at least as much within their power as within ours—and hence they are diligent in cultivating it; but still, they have not a single great painting to boast of, just because they are deficient in that objectivity of mind which is so directly indispensable in painting. They never get beyond a subjective point of view. It is quite in keeping with this that ordinary women have no real susceptibility for art at all; for Nature proceeds in strict sequence—non facit saltum. And Huarte in his Examen de ingenios para las scienzias—a book which has been famous for three hundred years—denies women the possession of all the higher faculties. The case is not altered by particular and partial exceptions; taken as a whole, women are, and remain, thorough-going Philistines, and quite incurable. Hence, with that absurd arrangement which allows them to share the rank and title of their husbands they are a constant stimulus to his ignoble ambitions. And, further, it is just because they are Philistines that modern society, where they take the lead and set the tone, is in such a bad way. Napoleon's saying—that women have no rank—should be adopted as the right standpoint in determining their position in society; and as regards their other qualities Chamfort[2] makes the very true remark: They are made to trade with our own weaknesses and our follies, but not with our reason. The sympathies that exist between them and men are skin-deep only, and do not touch the mind or the feelings or the character. They form the sexus sequior—the second sex, inferior in every respect to the first; their infirmities should be treated with consideration; but to show them great reverence is extremely ridiculous, and lowers us in their eyes. When Nature made two divisions of the human race, she did not draw the line exactly through the middle. These divisions are polar and opposed to each other, it is true; but the difference between them is not qualitative merely, it is also quantitative.

This is just the view which the ancients took of woman, and the view which people in the East take now; and their judgment as to her proper position is much more correct than ours, with our old French notions of gallantry and our preposterous system of reverence—that highest product of Teutonico-Christian stupidity. These notions have served only to make women more arrogant and overbearing; so that one is occasionally reminded of the holy apes in Benares, who in the consciousness of their sanctity and inviolable position, think they can do exactly as they please.

But in the West, the woman, and especially the lady, finds herself in a false position; for woman, rightly called by the ancients, sexus sequior, is by no means fit to be the object of our honor and veneration, or to hold her head higher than man and be on equal terms with him. The consequences of this false position are sufficiently obvious. Accordingly, it would be a very desirable thing if this Number-Two of the human race were in Europe also relegated to her natural place, and an end put to that lady nuisance, which not only moves all Asia to laughter, but would have been ridiculed by Greece and Rome as well. It is impossible to calculate the good effects which such a change would bring about in our social, civil and political arrangements. There would be no necessity for the Salic law: it would be a superfluous truism. In Europe the lady, strictly so-called, is a being who should not exist at all; she should be either a housewife or a girl who hopes to become one; and she should be brought up, not to be arrogant, but to be thrifty and submissive. It is just because there are such people asladies in Europe that the women of the lower classes, that is to say, the great majority of the sex, are much more unhappy than they are in the East. And even Lord Byron says:Thought of the state of women under the ancient Greeks—convenient enough. Present state, a remnant of the barbarism of the chivalric and the feudal ages—artificial and unnatural. They ought to mind home—and be well fed and clothed—but not mixed in society. Well educated, too, in religion—but to read neither poetry nor politics— nothing but books of piety and cookery. Music—drawing—dancing—also a little gardening and ploughing now and then. I have seen them mending the roads in Epirus with good success. Why not, as well as hay-making and milking?

The laws of marriage prevailing in Europe consider the woman as the equivalent of the man—start, that is to say, from a wrong position. In our part of the world where monogamy is the rule, to marry means to halve one's rights and double one's duties. Now, when the laws gave women equal rights with man, they ought to have also endowed her with a masculine intellect. But the fact is, that just in proportion as the honors and privileges which the laws accord to women, exceed the amount which nature gives, is there a diminution in the number of women who really participate in these privileges; and all the remainder are deprived of their natural rights by just so much as is given to the others over and above their share. For the institution of monogamy, and the laws of marriage which it entails, bestow upon the woman an unnatural position of privilege, by considering her throughout as the full equivalent of the man, which is by no means the case; and seeing this, men who are shrewd and prudent very often scruple to make so great a sacrifice and to acquiesce in so unfair an arrangement.

Consequently, whilst among polygamous nations every woman is provided for, where monogamy prevails the number of married women is limited; and there remains over a large number of women without stay or support, who, in the upper classes, vegetate as useless old maids, and in the lower succumb to hard work for which they are not suited; or else become filles de joie, whose life is as destitute of joy as it is of honor. But under the circumstances they become a necessity; and their position is openly recognized as serving the special end of warding off temptation from those women favored by fate, who have found, or may hope to find, husbands. In London alone there are 80,000 prostitutes. What are they but the women, who, under the institution of monogamy have come off worse? Theirs is a dreadful fate: they are human sacrifices offered up on the altar of monogamy. The women whose wretched position is here described are the inevitable set-off to the European lady with her arrogance and pretension. Polygamy is therefore a real benefit to the female sex if it is taken as a whole. And, from another point of view, there is no true reason why a man whose wife suffers from chronic illness, or remains barren, or has gradually become too old for him, should not take a second. The motives which induce so many people to become converts to Mormonism appear to be just those which militate against the unnatural institution of monogamy.

Moreover, the bestowal of unnatural rights upon women has imposed upon them unnatural duties, and, nevertheless, a breach of these duties makes them unhappy. Let me explain. A man may often think that his social or financial position will suffer if he marries, unless he makes some brilliant alliance. His desire will then be to win a woman of his own choice under conditions other than those of marriage, such as will secure her position and that of the children. However fair, reasonable, fit and proper these conditions may be, and the woman consents by foregoing that undue amount of privilege which marriage alone can bestow, she to some extent loses her honor, because marriage is the basis of civic society; and she will lead an unhappy life, since human nature is so constituted that we pay an attention to the opinion of other people which is out of all proportion to its value. On the other hand, if she does not consent, she runs the risk either of having to be given in marriage to a man whom she does not like, or of being landed high and dry as an old maid; for the period during which she has a chance of being settled for life is very short. And in view of this aspect of the institution of monogamy, Thomasius' profoundly learned treatise, de Concubinatu, is well worth reading; for it shows that, amongst all nations and in all ages, down to the Lutheran Reformation, concubinage was permitted; nay, that it was an institution which was to a certain extent actually recognized by law, and attended with no dishonor. It was only the Lutheran Reformation that degraded it from this position. It was seen to be a further justification for the marriage of the clergy; and then, after that, the Catholic Church did not dare to remain behind-hand in the matter.

There is no use arguing about polygamy; it must be taken as de facto existing everywhere, and the only question is as to how it shall be regulated. Where are there, then, any real monogamists? We all live, at any rate, for a time, and most of us, always, in polygamy. And so, since every man needs many women, there is nothing fairer than to allow him, nay, to make it incumbent upon him, to provide for many women. This will reduce woman to her true and natural position as a subordinate being; and the lady—that monster of European civilization and Teutonico-Christian stupidity—will disappear from the world, leaving only women, but no more unhappy women, of whom Europe is now full.

In India, no woman is ever independent, but in accordance with the law of Mamu, she stands under the control of her father, her husband, her brother or her son. It is, to be sure, a revolting thing that a widow should immolate herself upon her husband's funeral pyre; but it is also revolting that she should spend her husband's money with her paramours — the money for which he toiled his whole life long, in the consoling belief that he was providing for his children. Happy are those who have kept the middle course — medium tenuere beati.

The first love of a mother for her child is, with the lower animals as with men, of a purely instinctive character, and so it ceases when the child is no longer in a physically helpless condition. After that, the first love should give way to one that is based on habit and reason; but this often fails to make its appearance, especially where the mother did not love the father. The love of a father for his child is of a different order, and more likely to last; because it has its foundation in the fact that in the child he recognizes his own inner self; that is to say, his love for it is metaphysical in its origin.

In almost all nations, whether of the ancient or the modern world, even amongst the Hottentots, property is inherited by the male descendants alone; it is only in Europe that a departure has taken place; but not amongst the nobility, however. That the property which has cost men long years of toil and effort, and been won with so much difficulty, should afterwards come into the hands of women, who then, in their lack of reason, squander it in a short time, or otherwise fool it away, is a grievance and a wrong as serious as it is common, which should be prevented by limiting the right of women to inherit. In my opinion, the best arrangement would be that by which women, whether widows or daughters, should never receive anything beyond the interest for life on property secured by mortgage, and in no case the property itself, or the capital, except where all male descendants fail. The people who make money are men, not women; and it follows from this that women are neither justified in having unconditional possession of it, nor fit persons to be entrusted with its administration. When wealth, in any true sense of the word, that is to say, funds, houses or land, is to go to them as an inheritance they should never be allowed the free disposition of it. In their case a guardian should always be appointed; and hence they should never be given the free control of their own children, wherever it can be avoided. The vanity of women, even though it should not prove to be greater than that of men, has this much danger in it, that it takes an entirely material direction. They are vain, I mean, of their personal beauty, and then of finery, show and magnificence. That is just why they are so much in their element in society. It is this, too, which makes them so inclined to be extravagant, all the more as their reasoning power is low. Accordingly we find an ancient writer describing woman as in general of an extravagant nature—[Greek: Gynae to synolon esti dapanaeron Physei][2] But with men vanity often takes the direction of non-material advantages, such as intellect, learning, courage.

In the Politics Aristotle explains the great disadvantage which accrued to the Spartans from the fact that they conceded too much to their women, by giving them the right of inheritance and dower, and a great amount of independence; and he shows how much this contributed to Sparta's fall. May it not be the case in France that the influence of women, which went on increasing steadily from the time of Louis XIII., was to blame for that gradual corruption of the Court and the Government, which brought about the Revolution of 1789, of which all subsequent disturbances have been the fruit? However that may be, the false position which women occupy, demonstrated as it is, in the most glaring way, by the institution of the lady, is a fundamental defect in our social scheme, and this defect, proceeding from the very heart of it, must spread its baneful influence in all directions.

That woman is by nature meant to obey may be seen by the fact that every woman who is placed in the unnatural position of complete independence, immediately attaches herself to some man, by whom she allows herself to be guided and ruled. It is because she needs a lord and master. If she is young, it will be a lover; if she is old, a priest.

ON NOISE.

Kant wrote a treatise on The Vital Powers. I should prefer to write a dirge for them. The superabundant display of vitality, which takes the form of knocking, hammering, and tumbling things about, has proved a daily torment to me all my life long. There are people, it is true—nay, a great many people—who smile at such things, because they are not sensitive to noise; but they are just the very people who are also not sensitive to argument, or thought, or poetry, or art, in a word, to any kind of intellectual influence. The reason of it is that the tissue of their brains is of a very rough and coarse quality. On the other hand, noise is a torture to intellectual people. In the biographies of almost all great writers, or wherever else their personal utterances are recorded, I find complaints about it; in the case of Kant, for instance, Goethe, Lichtenberg, Jean Paul; and if it should happen that any writer has omitted to express himself on the matter, it is only for want of an opportunity.

This aversion to noise I should explain as follows: If you cut up a large diamond into little bits, it will entirely lose the value it had as a whole; and an army divided up into small bodies of soldiers, loses all its strength. So a great intellect sinks to the level of an ordinary one, as soon as it is interrupted and disturbed, its attention distracted and drawn off from the matter in hand; for its superiority depends upon its power of concentration—of bringing all its strength to bear upon one theme, in the same way as a concave mirror collects into one point all the rays of light that strike upon it. Noisy interruption is a hindrance to this concentration. That is why distinguished minds have always shown such an extreme dislike to disturbance in any form, as something that breaks in upon and distracts their thoughts. Above all have they been averse to that violent interruption that comes from noise. Ordinary people are not much put out by anything of the sort. The most sensible and intelligent of all nations in Europe lays down the rule, Never Interrupt! as the eleventh commandment. Noise is the most impertinent of all forms of interruption. It is not only an interruption, but also a disruption of thought. Of course, where there is nothing to interrupt, noise will not be so particularly painful. Occasionally it happens that some slight but constant noise continues to bother and distract me for a time before I become distinctly conscious of it. All I feel is a steady increase in the labor of thinking—just as though I were trying to walk with a weight on my foot. At last I find out what it is. Let me now, however, pass from genus to species. The most inexcusable and disgraceful of all noises is the cracking of whips—a truly infernal thing when it is done in the narrow resounding streets of a town. I denounce it as making a peaceful life impossible; it puts an end to all quiet thought. That this cracking of whips should be allowed at all seems to me to show in the clearest way how senseless and thoughtless is the nature of mankind. No one with anything like an idea in his head can avoid a feeling of actual pain at this sudden, sharp crack, which paralyzes the brain, rends the thread of reflection, and murders thought. Every time this noise is made, it must disturb a hundred people who are applying their minds to business of some sort, no matter how trivial it may be; while on the thinker its effect is woeful and disastrous, cutting his thoughts asunder, much as the executioner's axe severs the head from the body. No sound, be it ever so shrill, cuts so sharply into the brain as this cursed cracking of whips; you feel the sting of the lash right inside your head; and it affects the brain in the same way as touch affects a sensitive plant, and for the same length of time.

With all due respect for the most holy doctrine of utility, I really cannot see why a fellow who is taking away a wagon-load of gravel or dung should thereby obtain the right to kill in the bud the thoughts which may happen to be springing up in ten thousand heads—the number he will disturb one after another in half an hour's drive through the town. Hammering, the barking of dogs, and the crying of children are horrible to hear; but your only genuine assassin of thought is the crack of a whip; it exists for the purpose of destroying every pleasant moment of quiet thought that any one may now and then enjoy. If the driver had no other way of urging on his horse than by making this most abominable of all noises, it would be excusable; but quite the contrary is the case. This cursed cracking of whips is not only unnecessary, but even useless. Its aim is to produce an effect upon the intelligence of the horse; but through the constant abuse of it, the animal becomes habituated to the sound, which falls upon blunted feelings and produces no effect at all. The horse does not go any faster for it. You have a remarkable example of this in the ceaseless cracking of his whip on the part of a cab-driver, while he is proceeding at a slow pace on the lookout for a fare. If he were to give his horse the slightest touch with the whip, it would have much more effect. Supposing, however, that it were absolutely necessary to crack the whip in order to keep the horse constantly in mind of its presence, it would be enough to make the hundredth part of the noise. For it is a well-known fact that, in regard to sight and hearing, animals are sensitive to even the faintest indications; they are alive to things that we can scarcely perceive. The most surprising instances of this are furnished by trained dogs and canary birds.

It is obvious, therefore, that here we have to do with an act of pure wantonness; nay, with an impudent defiance offered to those members of the community who work with their heads by those who work with their hands. That such infamy should be tolerated in a town is a piece of barbarity and iniquity, all the more as it could easily be remedied by a police-notice to the effect that every lash shall have a knot at the end of it. There can be no harm in drawing the attention of the mob to the fact that the classes above them work with their heads, for any kind of headwork is mortal anguish to the man in the street. A fellow who rides through the narrow alleys of a populous town with unemployed post-horses or cart-horses, and keeps on cracking a whip several yards long with all his might, deserves there and then to stand down and receive five really good blows with a stick.

All the philanthropists in the world, and all the legislators, meeting to advocate and decree the total abolition of corporal punishment, will never persuade me to the contrary! There is something even more disgraceful than what I have just mentioned. Often enough you may see a carter walking along the street, quite alone, without any horses, and still cracking away incessantly; so accustomed has the wretch become to it in consequence of the unwarrantable toleration of this practice. A man's body and the needs of his body are now everywhere treated with a tender indulgence. Is the thinking mind then, to be the only thing that is never to obtain the slightest measure of consideration or protection, to say nothing of respect? Carters, porters, messengers—these are the beasts of burden amongst mankind; by all means let them be treated justly, fairly, indulgently, and with forethought; but they must not be permitted to stand in the way of the higher endeavors of humanity by wantonly making a noise. How many great and splendid thoughts, I should like to know, have been lost to the world by the crack of a whip? If I had the upper hand, I should soon produce in the heads of these people an indissoluble association of ideas between cracking a whip and getting a whipping.

Let us hope that the more intelligent and refined among the nations will make a beginning in this matter, and then that the Germans may take example by it and follow suit. Meanwhile, I may quote what Thomas Hood says of them[2]: For a musical nation, they are the most noisy I ever met with. That they are so is due to the fact, not that they are more fond of making a noise than other people—they would deny it if you asked them—but that their senses are obtuse; consequently, when they hear a noise, it does not affect them much. It does not disturb them in reading or thinking, simply because they do not think; they only smoke, which is their substitute for thought. The general toleration of unnecessary noise—the slamming of doors, for instance, a very unmannerly and ill-bred thing—is direct evidence that the prevailing habit of mind is dullness and lack of thought. In Germany it seems as though care were taken that no one should ever think for mere noise—to mention one form of it, the way in which drumming goes on for no purpose at all.

Finally, as regards the literature of the subject treated of in this chapter, I have only one work to recommend, but it is a good one. I refer to a poetical epistle in terzo rimo by the famous painter Bronzino, entitled De' Romori: a Messer Luca Martini. It gives a detailed description of the torture to which people are put by the various noises of a small Italian town. Written in a tragicomic style, it is very amusing. The epistle may be found in Opere burlesche del Berni, Aretino ed altri, Vol. II., p. 258; apparently published in Utrecht in 1771.

A FEW PARABLES.

In a field of ripening corn I came to a place which had been trampled down by some ruthless foot; and as I glanced amongst the countless stalks, every one of them alike, standing there so erect and bearing the full weight of the ear, I saw a multitude of different flowers, red and blue and violet. How pretty they looked as they grew there so naturally with their little foliage! But, thought I, they are quite useless; they bear no fruit; they are mere weeds, suffered to remain only because there is no getting rid of them. And yet, but for these flowers, there would be nothing to charm the eye in that wilderness of stalks. They are emblematic of poetry and art, which, in civic life—so severe, but still useful and not without its fruit—play the same part as flowers in the corn.

There are some really beautifully landscapes in the world, but the human figures in them are poor, and you had not better look at them.

The fly should be used as the symbol of impertinence and audacity; for whilst all other animals shun man more than anything else, and run away even before he comes near them, the fly lights upon his very nose.

Two Chinamen traveling in Europe went to the theatre for the first time. One of them did nothing but study the machinery, and he succeeded in finding out how it was worked. The other tried to get at the meaning of the piece in spite of his ignorance of the language. Here you have the Astronomer and the Philosopher.

Wisdom which is only theoretical and never put into practice, is like a double rose; its color and perfume are delightful, but it withers away and leaves no seed.

No rose without a thorn. Yes, but many a thorn without a rose.

A wide-spreading apple-tree stood in full bloom, and behind it a straight fir raised its dark and tapering head. Look at the thousands of gay blossoms which cover me everywhere, said the apple-tree; what have you to show in comparison? Dark-green needles! That is true, replied the fir, but when winter comes, you will be bared of your glory; and I shall be as I am now.

Once, as I was botanizing under an oak, I found amongst a number of other plants of similar height one that was dark in color, with tightly closed leaves and a stalk that was very straight and stiff. When I touched it, it said to me in firm tones: Let me alone; I am not for your collection, like these plants to which Nature has given only a single year of life. I am a little oak.

So it is with a man whose influence is to last for hundreds of years. As a child, as a youth, often even as a full-grown man, nay, his whole life long, he goes about among his fellows, looking like them and seemingly as unimportant. But let him alone; he will not die. Time will come and bring those who know how to value him.

The man who goes up in a balloon does not feel as though he were ascending; he only sees the earth sinking deeper under him.

There is a mystery which only those will understand who feel the truth of it.

Your estimation of a man's size will be affected by the distance at which you stand from him, but in two entirely opposite ways according as it is his physical or his mental stature that you are considering. The one will seem smaller, the farther off you move; the other, greater.

Nature covers all her works with a varnish of beauty, like the tender bloom that is breathed, as it were, on the surface of a peach or a plum. Painters and poets lay themselves out to take off this varnish, to store it up, and give it us to be enjoyed at our leisure. We drink deep of this beauty long before we enter upon life itself; and when afterwards we come to see the works of Nature for ourselves, the varnish is gone: the artists have used it up and we have enjoyed it in advance. Thus it is that the world so often appears harsh and devoid of charm, nay, actually repulsive. It were better to leave us to discover the varnish for ourselves. This would mean that we should not enjoy it all at once and in large quantities; we should have no finished pictures, no perfect poems; but we should look at all things in that genial and pleasing light in which even now a child of Nature sometimes sees them — some one who has not anticipated his aesthetic pleasures by the help of art, or taken the charms of life too early.

The Cathedral in Mayence is so shut in by the houses that are built round about it, that there is no one spot from which you can see it as a whole. This is symbolic of everything great or beautiful in the world. It ought to exist for its own sake alone, but before very long it is misused to serve alien ends. People come from all directions wanting to find in it support and maintenance for themselves; they stand in the way and spoil its effect. To be sure, there is nothing surprising in this, for in a world of need and imperfection everything is seized upon which can be used to satisfy want. Nothing is exempt from this service, no, not even those very things which arise only when need and want are for a moment lost sight of—the beautiful and the true, sought for their own sakes.

This is especially illustrated and corroborated in the case of institutions—whether great or small, wealthy or poor, founded, no matter in what century or in what land, to maintain and advance human knowledge, and generally to afford help to those intellectual efforts which ennoble the race. Wherever these institutions may be, it is not long before people sneak up to them under the pretence of wishing to further those special ends, while they are really led on by the desire to secure the emoluments which have been left for their furtherance, and thus to satisfy certain coarse and brutal instincts of their own. Thus it is that we come to have so many charlatans in every branch of knowledge. The charlatan takes very different shapes according to circumstances; but at bottom he is a man who cares nothing about knowledge for its own sake, and only strives to gain the semblance of it that he may use it for his own personal ends, which are always selfish and material.

Every hero is a Samson. The strong man succumbs to the intrigues of the weak and the many; and if in the end he loses all patience he crushes both them and himself. Or he is like Gulliver at Lilliput, overwhelmed by an enormous number of little men.

A mother gave her children Aesop's fables to read, in the hope of educating and improving their minds; but they very soon brought the book back, and the eldest, wise beyond his years, delivered himself as follows: This is no book for us; it's much too childish and stupid. You can't make us believe that foxes and wolves and ravens are able to talk; we've got beyond stories of that kind!

In these young hopefuls you have the enlightened Rationalists of the future.

A number of porcupines huddled together for warmth on a cold day in winter; but, as they began to prick one another with their quills, they were obliged to disperse. However the cold drove them together again, when just the same thing happened. At last, after many turns of huddling and dispersing, they discovered that they would be best off by remaining at a little distance from one another. In the same way the need of society drives the human porcupines together, only to be mutually repelled by the many prickly and disagreeable qualities of their nature. The moderate distance which they at last discover to be the only tolerable condition of intercourse, is the code of politeness and fine manners; and those who transgress it are roughly told—in the English phrase—to keep their distance. By this arrangement the mutual need of warmth is only very moderately satisfied; but then people do not get pricked. A man who has some heat in himself prefers to remain outside, where he will neither prick other people nor get pricked himself.

www.ingramcontent.com/pod-product-compliance
Lightning Source LLC
Chambersburg PA
CBHW080022130526
44591CB00036B/2574